FOG
A Collection of
Backscatter

FOG

A Collection of Backscatter

Brad Tipler, M.D.

Evil Humours Press

Manufactured in the United States of America
Library of Congress Catalog Card Number: 98-93833
ISBN: 0-9666738-0-8
Cover design: Pearl and Associates
Book design and production: Tabby House

Dr. Brad Tipler's column, "Backscatter,"
appears in *Diagnostic Imaging* magazine.

Dedication

For my mom and dad

Evil Humours Press, a division of
BMT Publishing
339 Yorkshire Avenue
Waynesboro, VA 22980
btipler@cfw.com

Foreword

Brad Tipler is a friend of mine, which gives me license to say he's a little off-center. This is a good thing, as what passes for the center in a field as innately conservative as radiology is pretty dry. The fringes, however, can get pretty darn interesting.

In the "Backscatter" columns that have appeared in Diagnostic Imaging over the past five years, Brad has written about subjects that, at face value, would appear too mundane to even mention. Like barium enemas. Or radiologists who whine too much. Or lightbox reading. With an imagination that sometimes borders on the bizarre, Brad finds the humor and occasionally the pathos to bring radiology alive in a way that no one else can. A barium blow-out is an occasion for sociological analysis. The weird stuff that radiologists think about when sitting in front of a batch of radiographs is put to words. It is not by being profound but by being human that this native of Alabama has become one of the best-known radiologists in the United States, and certainly the most widely read. His columns brighten the day of medical professionals for whom humorous writing is welcome relief from chest films, bone-headed ER docs, and HMOs.

As a magazine editor who sees a lot of bad writing by doctors, I can say with some authority that there's nothing tougher than writing something funny. I was so certain of his inevitable failure that it took some convincing for me to decide to give Brad a tryout as a writer. I'm glad I did. In the essays that follow, I think you'll find much that will amuse you, and maybe even something that will make you laugh out loud. And if pushing barium is your idea of illicit fun, this book will be downright riotous. I hope you enjoy it.

PETER OGLE, EDITOR
Diagnostic Imaging

Introduction

In 1993 I decided it would be fun to try my hand at writing. Encouraged by my family, I wrote a few short pieces about radiology. Because I had never done anything for publication, they took a lot of editing by my wife, a former English major.

Once I had them done, I looked through my journals to see which one might publish my style of work. I couldn't decide where I had the best chance of acceptance, so I just started at the top—*Diagnostic Imaging*. I figured if I was going to get rejected, it might as well be by the best radiology magazine first. Much to my surprise, the editor was willing to give my column a six-month trial. I've been writing it monthly ever since.

The main point of my column is to make people laugh. We do a lot of funny things in radiology, but we're usually too serious and busy to notice. Of course, I also try to sneak in my views on what is, and is not, important about our work.

This book is made up of most of the columns from 1993–1998. I played with the idea of arranging them by topics, but in the end decided on a chronologic order. Radiology is constantly changing. My column reflects what is happening in my life and practice when I am writing it, so the columns make a little more sense when read in order. Besides, who wants to read five essays in a row about the RSNA annual meeting in Chicago?

Thanks to Peter Ogle and all the folks at DI who have helped and supported my column. And, thanks to all of you who have taken the time to write or stop me at a meeting and comment on my work. It is really fun to hear from you.

BRAD TIPLER, M.D.

1993

We Have Met the Barium Enemy
and It Is Us

"Good morning. My name is Dr. Tipler. Your doctor has asked us to perform a barium enema on you. This is a test to evaluate your colon. You may have some discomfort but please do your best to hold the barium in. *Barium on!*"

I learned this speech as a resident. It takes less than thirty seconds to say, if you don't stop to breathe. Patients find it very informative, like a subway announcement. Some years later I had a conversation that went something like this:

Friend: "I had a BE."

Me: "How was it?"

Friend: "The room was dark. I had a watermelon up my behind. A guy came in mumbling a mile a minute. I heard the word *on* and then the watermelon exploded."

Me: "Didn't your radiologist introduce himself, explain the procedure, and answer questions?"

Friend: "No. But who wants to chat when you have a watermelon ticking inside of you?"

That's when I began thinking of the test as the Barium Enemy.

My primary goal is still to obtain optimal pictures as quickly as possible, but I now see myself as more of a coach, helping the patient through the exam. I talk to my patients before they're tipped. I sit down to talk to them, since sitting conveys a lack of urgency, even if I'm rushing like mad. After briefly explaining the exam, the video monitor and the balloon tip, I finish by asking them if they have any questions other than "How do I get out of this?"

BE techniques are like hospital committees: too numerous to count, but few are of much use. You should consider yourself lucky if you find one that consistently works. My personal favorite is a modification of Miller and Maglinte's "seven-pump" technique *(AJR,* Dec. 1982). Originally published as a technique to be done by technologists, the method is simple and reliable. The main modification I use is frequent fluoroscopy and filming of the sigmoid colon during filling. I do this out of hate. I loathe the sigmoid region. It has been responsible for most of my errors over the years. If and when I ever subspecialize, it will be in patients who have had sigmoidectomies.

Glucagon is always nearby. A lot of trees have been wasted debating the topic of IV versus subcutaneous administration. I inject 0.5 cc intravenously, then poke my 25-gauge needle through the other side of the vein and give the rest subcutaneously. It doesn't seem to hurt. This gives an immediate and prolonged effect, but then I'm a belt-and-suspenders man.

Some BEs are more fun than others. There is a certain aesthetic appeal to a high-contrast film from a good air study, particularly a decubitus view with really good grid alignment on a thin patient. But I live in a rural town—the land of milk and sausage—so I see many patients with "biscuit poisoning." Those folks just scatter those aesthetic photons all over the room.

The sheer number of "helpful products" available for BEs is amazing. When I was a resident you just filled the colon with barium. To add air, you put the bag on the floor to drain and then stepped on it. Next came the bulb, so you could slowly pump in air by hand—one of life's great little ideas. Then came high-density barium with emulsifiers, surface tension agents, and epoxy.

I particularly like the articles I have read about devices to inject compressed CO_2. A patient being hooked up to one of those devices must have a mental image of a helium balloon about to be inflated. Soon I'll be marketing my own "state-of-the-art coating machine" based on recycled hardware store paint shakers.

When my daughter had ENT surgery at a nearby teaching hospital, she was occasionally referred to as "the nose in room three." In my practice, I try to remember I am dealing with a person, not a "colon." Contrary to popular belief, a radiologist is allowed to touch patients. During the exam, I talk to my patients and put my hand on their shoulders to reassure them.

Encourage your patient throughout the exam. Acknowledge that the exam isn't your idea of something you would like to do on a Saturday night, but that you and the patient can get through it together.

Common enemies build unity. Help your patients face this one.

Behold the Future with Cosmic Radiology

My fifteen-year-old son and I have developed a whole new field of radiology, for which I envision subspecialty certification by the year 2000. It took only a boring ride down the interstate and a tabloid paper—the kind you laugh at in the supermarket checkout line—to spark our genius.

We noticed the apparently insatiable desire of some people to know more about themselves. Self-knowledge can be found on your palm, in tea leaves, stars, cards, pig entrails and a host of other equally logical places. It was an easy step to develop a highly accurate system for forecasting the future based entirely on body imaging. We call it cosmic roentgenology.

I plan a two-tier approach: one aimed at the general public and the other a highly regulated subspecialty within radiology.

My forthcoming book will describe how average daytime television junkies can, merely by checking out their X-rays from the local hospital, chart their futures. Viewers need only tape the appropriate radiograph on their TV screen and make a careful analysis based on my exorbitantly priced book that promises viewers the opportunity to *see all those things your doctor never sees.*

My system analyzes "critical metamorphic lines" on commonly obtained X-ray exams. These CMLs are correlated with your astrological sign to produce a totally reliable system on which to base the rest of your life. Detailed analysis of chest, skull, ankle, hand, wrist, feet, cervical spine, lumbar spine and abdominal X-rays will be available. Some areas of the body have already been subjected to scientific analysis and, where applicable, these data have been incorporated into CR methodology. The classic works in phrenology are equally valid when applied to the skull film, but far more precise.

Reflexology, a combination of phrenology and "this little piggy goes to market," also translates well from your foot to the viewbox. Palm reading may become obsolete.

Intuitively, certain areas of one's social and spiritual life correlate closely with specific anatomic regions. For example, the "longevity ratio" is an important factor for Pisces and Sagittarii when making long-range philosophical planning goals at or around the new moon. This ratio, based on the relation between the width of the chest and heart, has absolutely no parallel in tarot cards. In affairs d'amour, the ratio obviously affects long-term commitments.

Less intuitive, but equally reliable, is the "zone-de-ferment." This prominent homogeneous gray area in the right upper quadrant on abdominal films can, in Aquarii and some other astrological groups, be correlated with one's propensity to nightlife and gaiety.

My book will be richly illustrated throughout with little consideration for reality.

In the professional imaging arena, cosmic roentgenology offers a wealth of possibilities. Entire academic careers will be launched from the ensuing multiauthored research papers. New empires within large university departments can be established, giving "division chair" status to a whole new community of rising young stellar radiologists. The Society of Cosmic Roentgenology would add credibility to our cause and allow us to discuss current work and play golf at world-class resorts. As the father of cosmic roentgenology, I will, of course, make myself available for the CME lecture circuit, preferably at meetings in semitropical climes.

It won't all be a bed of roses. There will be turf battles with psychiatry, holistic practitioners, and housekeeping departments. But if we position ourselves astutely on the credentials committee, we should be able to fight off these invasions. Entrepreneurial types will probably set up private cosmic offices where standards may be less than professional. Initially, Medicare reimbursement may be a problem, but I think Bill and Hillary and the rest of their crowd in Washington may be just the folks to embrace this innovative, job-creating, low-capital medical advancement.

So keep your eye out for too-numerous-to-count multicolored brochures with address labels, bookplates, and various other priceless enticements arriving in your mail. In addition, you can look for a completely unbiased display at this year's RSNA scientific exhibits.

Me and the ACP: a Tick Among Fleas

The annual meeting of the American College of Physicians is to internists what the RSNA meeting is to radiologists: a multi-ring medical circus. That must be why I enjoyed being there. It's a good exercise to attend meetings outside our specialty. It changes your perspective, like watching "Bonanza" reruns dubbed in Japanese.

I believe I was the only radiologist at the ACP meeting in Washington, DC. There were plenty of strange looks when I introduced myself. I think they were looking for horns and a pitchfork—or perhaps they expected me to be wearing a Hawaiian print shirt.

The big event the first day was the keynote address by Vice President Al Gore. The ACP has formally endorsed a managed-care-style program. Internists are a primary-care specialty, so his talk had a certain "Let's win for the Gipper" quality, as opposed to the messages of impending doom you tend to hear at radiology meetings.

What I found particularly fascinating was something he didn't say. There were roughly 7,000 physicians waiting to hear Gore speak, who was thirty minutes late. When he finally arrived, the V.P. strode boldly to the podium and launched straight into his speech. Approximately 3,500 physician-hours had been wasted without an apology. He might as well have waved a big banner that said, "There's a new game in town, and you guys aren't on the team." It was payback time for all those hours America has lost in doctors' waiting rooms.

I attended several excellent sessions each day, but the talks are very different from those at radiology meetings. They can be rendered complete on audiotape, as there are few visual aids. A few sad black-and-white slides would occasionally be shown, the margins of which usually included the surface of the speaker's desk.

One neurologist did show some current images. He was particularly fond of MR angiography and he convinced me that I should move to the Northeast. Radiologists up there do an entire cranial MRI in five minutes and make four times as much as neurologists. To do an MRA they just push one button and the whole thing is done." It sounds like radiologists around Boston and the Lehigh Valley are in Nirvana.

This same speaker, like many others I have heard, tended to anthropomorphize imaging equipment. Non-radiologists often speak glowingly of "CT advances" or "amazing things seen on MRI"—like these machines do this stuff on their own and we're nothing more than large knobs on the front. Maybe this is another case of doing a job so well it just looks easy.

There was one striking similarity between the ACP and RSNA meetings. Many exhibits used the same time-tested, highly technical, professional techniques for marketing drugs and complex medical equipment:

Me: "I'm interested in that new drug that lowers blood pressure and eliminates GERD" (the acronym du jour for GE reflux).

Pretty young lady in tights: "Would you like some yogurt?"

Me: "I'm sorry. I thought this was Marko Drugs' booth."

PYLIT: "It is. Would you like a pocket knife?"

Me: "Do you have any literature on this drug?"

PYLIT: "Sure! Would you like me to put it in this handy carry-on bag that converts into a five-person tent?"

One aspect of the meeting was outstanding. I joined a small group program, a "college within the college," which began the evening before the main meeting. Thereafter, seven of us met over breakfast and in the afternoon each day of the meeting to share what we had learned. I enjoyed getting to know the participants and learned a lot. I will be making a concerted effort to bring a similar program to the 1994 RSNA meeting. (Update 98—I tried. They weren't interested.)

Please don't show this article to your friends in internal medicine. I always thought of the term "fleas" as a sort of humorous compliment, focusing on the unceasing attention to minute details that seems to characterize good internists. They don't appear to have the same appreciation for the term. Next year the ACP meeting is in Miami and I hope to go, but that town is dangerous enough without 7,000 internists gunning for me.

Biting the Hands that Feed Us

As a scientist (of sorts), I find the classification of various organisms both interesting and useful. If you are occasionally inclined to bite the hand that feeds you, referring physicians can be fun to categorize.

This ubiquitous family has two major genera; the genus *Friendosus* and the genus *Paineousgiuteus*. The former is typically nonpathogenic while the latter is frequently toxic—even with brief exposure.

Members of genus *Paineousgiuteus* are usually nosocomial pathogens. An M.D. vanity plate is almost pathognomonic. The degree of toxicity is often proportional to the length of their postgraduate training, although many members seem inherently caustic.

Paineousgiuteus arrogant is the dominant member. Members of this group have frequently metastasized from a "major medical center." Whenever possible they travel with an entourage of lesser beings. At frequent intervals they proclaim as loudly as possible their disdain for genus *Roenigenologist*. They seem totally unaware of the old adage, "Two heads are better than one."

A more insidious problem is attributable to the species *P. filmhoarder.* This seemingly benign group appears to place some intrinsic value on X-ray films. Film jackets are frequently found in their offices, car trunks, homes, etc. On questioning, a childhood history of baseball card collecting or shoplifting can usually be elicited.

P. filmshifter is a closely related variant of *P. filmhoarder.* Rather than taking the whole package home, they separate the films, jacket and reports, spreading the various components around your department.

Seen only intermittently is the species *P. heretowhine,* the members of which begin every visit with the phrase "I don't want to complain" before beginning to complain. Occasionally they will actually point out a significant problem over which you have some control. I find "I'll look right into it" (spoken approximately two octaves lower than your normal voice) is an effective way to deal with them.

The *P. night owl* wants all types of exams twenty-four hours a day. Members of this species seem oblivious to the concept of circadian rhythms and fail to appreciate what effect this may have on the exams produced.

The genus *Friendosus* is generally a much more tolerable group. Typically they form a symbiotic relationship with your department rather than a parasitic one. Feed this group donuts.

Friendosus debators are usually fun to have around. They value your opinion but have one of their own. Having read and considered your report they come down to "talk about it." Such conversations are always informative, usually enjoyable, often instructive, but occasionally frustrating—like talking to your parents.

The *F. clinicalis* is closely related to the *F. debator* above. The distinguishing feature is their unrelenting reliance on clinical findings in the face of overwhelming imaging evidence to the contrary. I particularly admire the intelligent members of this group, and not infrequently find them to be right.

F. statmeister really values your opinion. So much so that they want every test done immediately and the results phoned to them. An expensive instant replay dictating system makes this species easier to satisfy.

The pursuit of knowledge sets the members of the species *F. learners* apart. Whenever they have an interesting or challenging case, they want to go over your findings and conclusions for their own edification. You typically learn something too in the process, and the patient profits as well. When someone in your family gets sick, you probably send them to this subtype. Their only drawback is an uncanny ability to appear in the middle of a busy fluoro schedule.

Always wanting to add one more obscure entity to any list of differential diagnoses is the mark of the *F. but-what-abouts*. Unfortunately, this species may crossbreed with genus *Roentgenologist*.

The *F life-of-riley* is a quaint group. Its members are always telling you how much they envy your job because they think you still work nine-to-five—even though your conversations with them usually take place at 2:00 A.M.

As with any system of classification, this one is probably incomplete. If in the course of your work you should identify additional biotypes, send them in for addition to the list.

Aberrant Behavior in Abundance at RSNA

Ongoing research of subjects attending the RSNA meeting has provided valuable information on the behavior of those involved in medical imaging, according to Dr. Darb Relpit, director of the Behavioral Research Institute in Staunton, Virginia. In an interview with *Diagnostic Imaging,* Relpit discloses some of his findings about normal and aberrant RSNA behavior.

DI: The existence of your secret committee, and its ongoing research at the RSNA meeting has recently come to light. What are the implications of this work?

Re/pit: I assure you, ours is not a secret committee, it is "unlisted." Had anyone asked before about our committee, its existence would not have been denied. The applications of our work are varied, from equipment design to management decisions.

DI: What is the makeup of your committee?

Re/pit: It has evolved over time. Initially just a group of researchers, we now include representatives from the hotels, bus lines, McCormick Place and the program committee.

DI: What are your goals?

Re/pit: Briefly stated, we hope to show how people who have chosen medical imaging as a career respond to both routine and unusual stress situations, and whether their response pattern differs from those outside that arena.

DI: Can you give us some specific examples of your projects without jeopardizing ongoing investigations?

Re/pit: We're very proud of our bus projects. An early experiment involved the intermittent use of drivers who had recently arrived in Chicago from Bozeman, Montana; they'd never been to Chicago before the start of the RSNA meeting. We've also tried various unannounced changes in the bus routes and timetables. We've also tested how many times a long line of attendees will watch empty buses go by before they get mad and take a cab.

DI: How do the hotels enter into the program?

Re/pit: The hotels represent a high degree of control for us. We typically manipulate about five percent of the reservations. We might send you the name of the wrong hotel so that when you check in they have "never heard of you." When members of the same radiology group reserve rooms near each other, we often cancel one room and suggest they "double up."

My personal favorite is placing an elaborate welcome basket in the room with the wrong name on it, as if it were delivered by mistake. We have found the radiologists usually eat the fruit and always drink the wine. Equipment folks just change the card and send the basket to a radiologist.

DI: You mentioned McCormick Place had a seat on your committee. Where do they fit in?

Re/pit: Haven't you been there? McCormick Place is the ultimate human maze, a behaviorist's dream. We can place both positive and negative reinforcers wherever we want. The expansion into McCormick Place North was our brainstorm. Working closely with the program committee we can bounce people back and forth all day long. Traffic controllers in the connecting hallway allow very close monitoring of all selected subjects. Of course we pick our subjects closely; its okay to play "Ping-Pong"—our nomenclature for frequent trips between the two buildings—with a healthy young resident all week, but we have to be careful with the older guys.

DI: Do the slide projection personnel work with your committee?

Re/pit: I really can't say.

DI: Is that the full extent of your current work?

Re/pit: Well, those are some of the big projects, but we have a lot of small ones. Take, for example, the "number of attendees," which is a totally fictitious number, like "the number of burgers served" at McDonald's. We just keep pushing it up, and no one questions it.

We plant stooges in some lectures who take a flash picture of every slide. Amazingly, no one stops them.

One year we printed the same daily paper four days in a row, changing only the page order from day to day. People read it every day!

DI: Do you have any new projects on line for this year?

Re/pit: I don't want to bias our results by giving out specifics. But I can tell you that we've added the Chicago Food Servers Union to our committee this year.

Holding Hands: the Healing Touch

Holding hands is an interesting phenomenon. My wife and I like to hold hands. Before they reached their teen-age years, my kids would hold my hand. Now they are reluctant to be seen in the same city with me.

Many young people hold hands in shopping malls. Judging from the way they are dressed—no shoelaces, shirts inside-out, baseball caps on backwards—I suspect they're lost and trying to help each other find an exit.

I'm not a real touchy-feely kind of person. A few years ago our church had a two-day men's seminar conducted by a noted author of men's awareness books. Interspersed throughout the two days were various types of exercises designed to loosen us up, like foot massage and free-form dancing. I found I don't loosen well.

Nevertheless, over the past few years I've made an effort to use holding hands in my radiology practice. I suspect reading "A Piece of My Mind" regularly in *JAMA* had something to do with it. Many of the contributors to that column mention or refer to "a healing touch" in one form or another.

My own image associated with that phrase used to be one of a TV evangelist banging people on the ear or forehead. I don't remember much emphasis on the use of touch in medical school. The primary touching emphasized in radiology residency is with lead gloves and long skinny needles.

I decided some years ago that—when it seemed appropriate—I would make a conscious effort to touch patients as I talked with them. Initially, little old ladies confined to stretchers were easiest. It is very easy to rest your hand on theirs while you explain a procedure or take a brief history.

I began by putting my hand on their shoulder but quickly realized holding hands was just as easy. Over the years I have become more comfortable with this form of patient contact and it requires less conscious effort.

Most patients like it when you hold their hand while talking with them; they appreciate your undivided attention. Sometimes this is easier said than done. I still find it very hard to use touch on young men, particularly the muscle-bound macho types. True, I work out most mornings at a gym, but these guys who look as if they put real weights on the ends of the barbells still intimidate me. Here again, the problem is usually mine, not the patient's.

Sometimes this can get you into trouble in unexpected ways. You ask "What brings you to the doctor?" and a long discourse ensues on Cousin Lisa's old Ford and the problem it had starting that morning, 'cause it was cold and it never does start well when the temperature drops below 45 degrees. One patient told me not to touch her because "we are both electric, but opposite charges."

There are a lot of jokes in radiology about physical contact between professionals, both doctors and technologists. Most of these center around the dark room. That is not the healing touch but "the incriminating touch."

Some people assume a radiology department has to be cold and impersonal. With that underlying assumption, it becomes very easy to be more attentive to your equipment than your patient. So, our departments usually are "cold" (accentuated by thin gowns designed for exhibitionists) but they don't have to be impersonal. In fact, every patient wants compassionate caregivers irrespective of which department in the hospital is involved.

The practice of radiology doesn't offer many opportunities for patient contact. My partners and I believe interaction with patients is important and we try to maximize the patient exposure—to us, not radiation. There is no question that patients notice the amount of time and concern both physicians and technologists give them.

The healing touch is equally available to all healthcare providers if they choose to use it. Even in radiology there is some truth to the saying, "No one cares how much you know, until they know how much you care."

I Got the Hillary-and-Her-Task-Force Blues

Over the past few years I have developed a taste for country-western music. Two of our CT techs are country-music fans, so whenever I go to the scanner to review a study, I hear lots of pickin' and twangin'. The sound sort of grows on you over time, like a canker sore. I'm not as sure I'll ever get used to female technologists chewing tobacco at work, though.

While there is a wide variety of country music, most songs share a few common themes. Male singers moan about the gal who left them, problems with the demon rum, and their relationships with various domestic and/or farm animals. Female country singers sing more about falling in and out of love, particularly with bad, rum-drinking men.

This music has had its effect on me. Since turning forty, I've begun to look at my options and how they affect my future. The current unrest in healthcare has increased my introspection. Apparently, I'm not alone in this. Middle-aged physicians across the United States are feeling the hit.

The impact of the uncertainty caused by healthcare reform combined with the usual self-doubts of mid-career professionals is like getting stuck with tumor board at the last minute—and then finding out it's a case you missed initially. At a time in my career when it is normal to wonder whether I'm on the right road, Hillary and her task force are out there digging potholes and putting up detour signs.

A few weeks ago all these ambiguous feelings fell into place. I decided I should become a country music star. The pay is good and there's no night call, just last call. I can't sing, but that doesn't seem to be a problem. Of course, a good song comes from experience, so I've taken some common themes, added some personal experience and written songs for my first album.

My first single may be "It's Hard to Court a Woman With Yellow Barium on Your Shoes." Or perhaps "My Baby Got Tired of Night Call, So She's Calling It a Night." These songs cry out with the loneliness of radiology.

While a tune like "My Favorite Nonionic is Johnny Walker Red" may not have universal appeal, who could resist "It's Hard to Push a Catheter When You're Stone-Cold Sober" or "Readin' Nucs Is Easy When You Read 'Em With Jim Beam."

Some songs address the every day stresses of radiology. "It's Friday Afternoon and a Swollen Leg Is Headed My Way" will send me straight to the top of the charts. Technologists around the world will be humming "I Got a Cross-Table C-Spine To Clear and the Rads Are Talkin' Football." And what radiologist can't identify with "I-Got-the-Halfway-Through-My-Father-in-law's-BE-and-I-Just-Blew-a-Tube Blues."

Senior radiologists will identify with "I Wanna Go Back To the Good Ole Days When Specialists Were Special." Too many of us know the pain of "I Lost My Buddy In a Turf Battle—He Was Nuked By a Cardiologist."

A couple of family-oriented songs should help to boost sales. "There Ain't Nothin' Good on the Tube Tonight, So How 'Bout We Go Get Our Heads X-rayed?" appeals to all ages. "No Need to Check, Ain't No Way She's Pregnant" also has that special family quality.

Writing lyrics about animals is a little tougher when you come from a radiology background. "We Got a Land Whale Stuck In Our CT Scanner" doesn't have quite the emotional appeal of a song about lonesome doggies on the trail. I did come up with one heartfelt lullaby, "Without My Truck, My Dog and My Baby, My Viewbox Is One Bulb Short."

When I think about such a major career change, it's easy to start day-dreaming. It's fun to imagine a heartwrencher like "I Wore My Cowboy Buckle To Work, and Now I'm Stuck To the MRI," playing in the background as a list of hits scrolls across the TV screen on a late night cable ad. Or how about "They Took Away My Scanner and Left Me For Dead"? I think that's what I'll sing at the Grand Ole Opry.

No doubt some of you are dealing with similar forks in the road of life (hey, another song idea), and although I've chosen country music, there are plenty of other options. America is probably ready for a revival of Roller Derby, and with twenty jobs per team ....

1994

What Will the RSNA Think of Next?

I just got back from my annual pilgrimage to Chicago. Every year I go there to reacquaint myself with the joys of waiting in line in subzero weather to ride a bus in heavy city traffic.

In 1992, I stayed at the luxurious Drake Hotel. You know it's a first-class hotel because it has warming lights where you stand in line for the bus. I felt like a McDonald's french fry waiting to be salted.

This time I was late in turning in my registration. Do not let this happen to you. I ended up in a dubious part of town in a little room with a sliding glass balcony door, on which was mounted a large dead bolt with a bold sign warning me to "keep this door locked at all times." My room was on the fourteenth floor.

I really do like our annual RSNA meeting, though. The scientific exhibits are my favorite part and this year brought a major innovation. In the past, I would spend three days at the meeting and end up with six or seven CME credits. This year you could log in electronically each thirty minutes in the scientific exhibits for CME credit. That's plenty of time to go get a soda, visit the bathroom and call home.

The scientific exhibits vary from ingenious to absurd. It has never really occurred to me to do an air contrast upper GI on a rat, but then I am your basic small-town radiologist. Still, I can spend hours sidestepping down the aisles and never seem to cover it all.

I have some questions, though. What do all the people who photograph each scientific exhibit do with the slides? Haven't they seen *Radio-graphics,* the greatest hits collection of the RSNA meeting? Some of the exhibits are hard enough to read as is; it's hard to imagine how they look on a 35 mm slide. Second, does anyone ever look at diagrams of molecules?

The acromegalic brother of the scientific exhibit is the technical exhibit, that pot of gold at the end of the RSNA rainbow.

This year I applied to the Technical Exhibits Committee for a booth to sell my "X-rays-R-Us" T-shirts, the profits of which go to charity. They turned me down because my exhibit was "not related to radiology education." I'd never thought before about how kind it is for all those companies to spend millions of dollars on "education." Of course, I had to fight the crowds getting educated at the industrial wheel manufacturer's booth and the various leasing and financial companies teaching me about private financing for medical equipment vendors.

My town is in the midst of building a new community hospital—possibly one of the last in the United States, given the current climate—so for the past two RSNA meetings I have spent a lot of time looking at equipment. It's like Christmas shopping with someone else's money.

When cruising the commercial exhibits I concentrate on the new equipment and technical advances. At the same time, my other cerebral hemisphere (the slightly warped one) is focusing on other aspects of the exhibit. For instance, last year GE clearly won the best elevator music award, but this year its booth switched to synthesizer-produced pseudo dance music. No doubt this cost them some sales.

Like most radiologists, I enjoy the tricky visual sales techniques and technical developments featured at the RSNA meeting. The Phantom Laboratory took a relatively mundane product like radiology phantoms and created an eye-catching exhibit. Siemens had a pair of angiomen made from colorful graphics and a variety of digital angio images that looked great. Voxel introduced the Voxbox, a new film viewer for special holographic images on film-a definite nominee for the "Really Neat to Look At But I Can't Believe It Will Sell" award.

Some of the most intense educational experiences at the RSNA take place outside McCormick Place. Shimadzu had a terrific after-hours seminar featuring an amazing variety of food, and boy can those Shimadzu folks polka!

For those of you attending the RSNA next year, let me give you one last tip on how to really enjoy your trip to Chicago. Around July, request replacement bids from the major vendors on several big pieces of equipment.

The Clinton Plan: Off With Their Heads!

I have trouble understanding politics. Healthcare reform is a perfect example.

It is obvious there are problems with our healthcare system. But physicians are taking heat that should be shared. Access to healthcare for the homeless, jobless, uneducated and working poor is a growing problem. But I wonder if they wouldn't prefer access to jobs, housing, education and a decent salary, the provision of which might make healthcare less of a problem.

My small-town practice provides very sophisticated, complex care that was unimaginable when I entered medicine nineteen years ago. Has the housing system improved this much in two decades? Is education so remarkably advanced? Do rap music and Madonna hold a candle to Motown, the Beatles and the Rolling Stones?

When I listen to Hillary Rodham Clinton talk about healthcare I am reminded of the wonderful medical illustrator, Frank Netter. His paintings are remarkable for their clarity, their ability to simplify a complex subject.

But the pictures are not real. If all your knowledge of medicine and the human anatomy comes from Netter-grams you will be in deep guano when you have to deal with real human beings suffering from real diseases. So I find it surprising that our healthcare system is being reformed by folks with no more experience than the Marx brothers.

I have to hand it to Mrs. Clinton, though; this new system she has come up with is a surprise. I have not actually read the proposal, but I have heard about it on TV. It does not seem like a system designed by those who will use it. As a physician I have a lot of trouble accepting a system of healthcare reform that relies heavily on "decapitation."

At first, I was shocked at how openly she discusses this approach, and how easily the press and public have accepted it. Once I got over my initial astonishment, I've come to see some merit in the idea.

There is an historical precedent for such a radical proposal. About two hundred years ago a Frenchman named Robespierre tried to reinvent government in France using the decapitation method. His system was initially popular with the masses, though not with those to whom it was applied. They didn't have much time to complain, however.

I suspect that, like the French revolutionaries, those in Washington who are reforming the healthcare system expect to be shielded from the unpleasant aspects of their system. Interestingly, when Robespierre became a "consumer" at the guillotine, the reform ended.

The cynic in me was certain the Clintons would produce a fast-talking shell game with a lot of goodies being passed out to voters now and a massive bill coming due in about ten years—just like Medicare. I didn't realize how tough Hillary Rodham Clinton is. Widespread decapitation will cut this nation's healthcare costs dramatically in a very short time.

I feared the task force would avoid the toughest question facing healthcare today: how to limit care. Physicians need to be given the authority or the guidelines to withhold tests or treatment they believe inappropriate, without fear of reprisal. Decapitation certainly takes care of that.

Tort reform was another issue I thought would be avoided. The new system makes that easy—we just make the American Bar Association one big PPO. Who could argue with a special reduced rate for decapitating lawyers?

Every day I am swamped with more information on how to cope with the coming reform. The ACR keeps sending letters and information packets on possible reform issues. A whole new industry has developed to capitalize on the fear.

There are courses on how to cope with the coming changes, how to survive the changes, how to profit from the changes, how to "keep your head" in the new healthcare system. Now that I know what's coming, I may start reading this stuff.

When the task force on healthcare reform was first announced I was upset by the lack of physician input. But now I realize that this French Revolution in healthcare could only be the work of lawyers.

Dirty Power and Other Service Rep Diversions

Given the complexity of Chicago's McCormick maze, it is not surprising that at least once every RSNA I find myself in the wrong lecture hall. After all, the RSNA attendance is just over three times the population of my hometown.

Usually I stumble into a detailed discussion of the imaging characteristics of a hemangiothingoma. I saw one of those at the AFIP and that's the only one I'll ever see, so I leave. I prefer the bread-and-butter review courses and updates—they're both good and plentiful at our annual meeting.

This last year I somehow ended up in a special session for equipment service personnel on the current revision of NEMA-JAVA Document 10W40, "Standard approach to user dissatisfaction with imaging equipment, 3 Ed." As I listened to the moderator quote from the document it was literally deja vu all over again.

From the introduction . . . *and so realizing the dependency of medical imaging on perception, the service technician's time is often more efficiently spent changing the dissatisfied user's perception of the equipment versus the actual manipulation/modification/repair of said equipment.*

There is a logical progression through which one should attempt to alleviate the perception of a problem. Of course this depends on with which user you are interfacing.

I was hooked. People who interface with others are so entertaining.

Typically you will first deal with a technologist. The best initial approach is to question the experience of the operator. This works best if you interface with a senior technologist who is no longer a frequent operator.

The speaker then suggested this could be developed into a long conversation about the decline in the quality of radiologic technology training in the last decade, thus diverting attention from the initial complaint.

If the operator error approach fails or is considered inappropriate, misdirecting the user's attention to a different piece of equipment is a good backup. Because it is involved in almost every imaging technique, the processor is the logical choice. This can often be suggested on the initial request for service even before one visits the site or inspects the machine.

The speaker pointed out the usefulness of this approach as a delaying tactic if an immediate service visit would be inconvenient: *Just tell them you had the same problem a week ago and it turned out to be the processor. That will put them in a tailspin for at least a few hours while they tear it apart and reassemble it.*

When dealing with equipment that is computer-based, one cannot overlook the fact that all such equipment requires electricity. This dependence is a useful ally. A wide variety of equipment shortcomings can be attributed to "a dirty power source" with complete impunity. To complicate the diversion one should next ask, "what is the humidity in this room?" Outside of the MRI lab it is rare for anyone to know what the humidity measures.

Odd that I've never had a sales rep tell me I needed pristine power.

Fielding a problem raised by a radiologist often requires a different approach. At smaller institutions a reference such as "They do it this way at The University and they aren't complaining" may be all you need to say When applicable, suggesting they buy the "top-of-the-line" model next time can be equally intimidating.

Practicing near a university, I hear this one a lot. I wonder if they ever tell the university folks, "They do it this way out in the country."

Actually repairing the equipment sometimes becomes unavoidable. In such cases the incident can still be used to your advantage. Once the repair is complete tell the customer that you had to "replace a board." Reiterate how fortunate the customer is to have had a service contract since these boards cost $5 million each.

Ultrasound machines are a real bargain since each one apparently contains $50 million worth of boards.

Before leaving the department it is also useful to mention that the newer version of said equipment has just been released, and such problems have been completely eliminated. Unfortunately, the "architecture" of their machine does not allow an upgrade.

When I got home I asked one of our service reps about this manual. He smiled and said that as far as he could remember he had never seen it.

Hospital Voices are All Around Us

Our department is never quiet. We are constantly barraged by hospital voices. My office is just off the main hall of our department, so I hear our fluoro techs each morning as they escort patients past my door. They deliver a canned talk, which I think of as the Morning Laxative Report.

Technologist: "You've never had a BE before? Have you been doing that miserable prep for the last two days? How 'bout those laxatives last night, did they work for you?"

Patient: "Work? I was up all night."

Unattached to faces, hospital voices come at you from all angles. Usually we tune them out, but if you listen carefully they can be pretty entertaining.

The dominant voice is the hospital paging operator. She sits next to the front door of the hospital, manning her powerful Briggs & Stratton MD8O switchboard with her paging headset clamped across her bouffant hairdo. She is always friendly—exactly the kind of person you want to see when you walk into a hospital.

There is an unwritten rule about paging operators. They must have the strongest regional accent of anyone in the hospital. In the South this means a slow, eloquent Southern drawl. Our own operator can increase the number of syllables in every word by a factor of two. Rigor mortis often sets in before the phrase "Code blue in room 257" can be repeated three times. It is a classic Southern voice.

Two years ago our hospital put in a direct access paging system. You just pick up any phone in the hospital, dial 77, and you're on the air. If you get a kick out of voices, this is like going from local channels to a satellite system on your TV. The variety is endless.

For patients, the system is a real treat. Now every sick person in the hospital can be awakened at 2:00 A.M. by someone who thinks you have to yell into the phone to be heard throughout the hospital. Critical healthcare data such as "Ruth, bring a bucket to room 457,' is no longer delayed by finding Ruth first.

By far the most interesting voices are those of my cohorts in crime—physicians. I have noticed a nearly universal pathologic process in our profession: Dictaphone Voice (DV). It is particularly rampant in radiology. Sadly, on an average day I spend more time holding a Dictaphone than holding my wife.

I haven't yet figured out whether DV is genetically or environmentally determined. More research will probably reveal a multifactorial process.

Professional transcriptionists have known of this affliction for years, though I have never seen it labeled. Although each radiologist develops a particular tone and cadence, there are three classic types of DV sufferers. Some radiologists step on the accelerator when they dictate, and their words become a blur of syllables. Except for an occasional breath, there are no pauses between words. These folks spend three times longer than necessary to contemplate a film, and then try to dictate the whole report in the time it takes to sneeze.

Others mumble as if they're telling a secret. Maybe these radiologists were overly chastised during their residencies. Or maybe it has to do with their toilet training.

Yet another group are the enunciators. They sound like first-grade teachers, phonetically instructing children how to read. Ev-er-y word is spo-ken clear-ly, slow-ly and with em-pha-sis on each syl-la-ble. The monotone is another common symptom of DV.

At the viewbox DV is a relatively benign process that is primarily a problem for the listener, like heavy metal music. But when the pathology surfaces away from the viewbox, it can cause problems.

My own children alerted me to the most common case. They have kindly pointed out that whenever I leave a message on an answering machine my voice "gets funny." You can imagine the depth of my despair when I realized how many people probably already know I suffer from DV—the afflicted is always the last to know.

My family also pointed out how obvious it is when someone is speaking with Dictaphone Voice. When you shift into that tone, the listener knows that your brain is on autopilot. DV is a chronic disease, and I know of no cure. The best advice I can give is not to use it in the bedroom.

Oh To Be Smilin' and Dialin' Again

As a resident I whined constantly to my wife about how much harder I was working than when in medical school or college. It was the truth, and it was a better way to gain sympathy than admitting I had been loafing for the last eight years.

Of course once you get into *private practice* everything is peaches and cream: great hours, huge salary, continuing education courses in exotic places. I couldn't wait to finish my residency. Like headache patients in the pre-CT era who wanted a pneumoencephalogram, only in retrospect did I realize how dumb I was.

Residencies haven't changed much in the last decade, other than having to learn about three times the information in the same amount of time. As residents we thought we did about ninety percent of the "real work" and chastised the faculty for their life of leisure. The faculty regularly told us how their work would go faster without us, the yoke around their necks. Neither group was in danger of succumbing to overwork.

The CT resident spent the day at the scanner console reviewing the request, programming the study, reviewing the images, and so forth. We used to drive the technologists mad with our dialin' and smilin'.

"That pancreas looks suspicious to me. Let's give him a bolus of contrast and run through the entire abdomen with 1.5 mm cuts."

At the time I didn't realize what a luxury I was enjoying. The real magnitude of my oversight hit me with the introduction of MRI.

We got our magnet a few years ago. I had been reading articles and seeing RSNA exhibits in Chicago for several years. Our purchase price included a basic course for each radiologist (and probably enough profit to send the salesman's four kids to college). I went to an additional course before the machine arrived. Initially, we had an overreading service and we made sure our newest partner was well trained in MRI. I thought we were well prepared, but then so did our fleet at Pearl Harbor.

The problem is time. In a general practice there is no time for someone to sit at the scanner all day and fiddle around. I volunteered to spend a month or two at the university learning MRI, while the group mailed me my paychecks. My partners declined.

Our new partner designed lots of protocols and I learned to read the routine images. But anyone can learn to read the images. One thing that defines a radiologist is an intuitive understanding of the physics underlying a given imaging modality. For me, that intuitive grasp of MRI has come slower than a Medicare payment. This problem isn't entirely my fault since, like Medicare, as soon as I begin to understand MRI, it changes.

I recently took a bold step—my partners called it insane—and signed up for a four-day MRI physics course. The course consisted of thirty-two hours of physics lectures give by Dr. Emanuel Kanal. Naturally, the course was in Orlando. After eight hours of lectures you can go back to your hotel room and read about all the fun things in town other people are doing.

On my flight south I devised strategies for remaining awake during the ordeal ahead of me. How does one not sleep through eight hours of physics a day? It seemed an impossible task. Fortunately, I was unaware of two critical facts: Dr. Kanal is goofier than I am, and he is the best teacher I've ever had.

He has many unique qualifications for teaching MRI, the most important being that he has three elbows in each arm. If you have not heard Dr. Kanal speak, you may doubt the importance of this anatomic aberration. Without seeing it yourself, it's difficult to picture how someone can physically display the simultaneous process of TI recovery and T2 decay, much less make the process intuitive. Imagine watching a silent film of Charlie Chaplin directing traffic with the dubbed voice of a rabbi and you'll be on the right track.

During the course I learned that we were hearing an abridged version of a program Dr. Kanal teaches in Pittsburgh. Eventually, I'll attend the full course, although I'm not sure even he can make eighty straight hours of physics nonlethal. In the meantime, I'll continue trying to master MRI at work, since (to quote the comic strip philosopher Dick Tracy) "He who controls magnetism, controls the world."

Who Are the People in Your Hallways?

Every department has "hall people," those patients sitting in wheelchairs and lying on stretchers around your department, coming or going for exams.

"Young man, do you work here?"

I realize immediately this is an unusually perceptive little lady tied in a wheelchair outside my office. True, she hasn't noticed my scrub suit, white coat and hospital name tag, but nobody is perfect—and I like that adjective "young."

"Yes ma'am, I do. Can I help you with something?"

"That young man back there just tried to kill me."

It is important to talk to the people in your hallways. They need the reassurance, and you need the feedback. The older folks in particular can be very forthright in their criticism of your department and personnel. Of course, you have to take things with a grain of salt, unless you think some of your techs really are torturing patients.

There is an endless variety of facial expressions in the hall. Some people seem indignant, as if it is our fault they're sick, hospitalized and having some miserable test. Although smiling at these people rarely evokes a response from them, you'll feel better for doing it.

Many patients seem uncomfortable in our hallways, not in pain, but socially awkward—as if sitting half-naked among a group of strangers with a bag of urine in your lap is unusual.

Some are nervous about what is going to happen to them; others are relieved that it's over.

"Excuse me, I'm scheduled for a BeeEee. Does that mean I'm going to have to drink that awful barium?"

"Well, no, sir. The good news is you won't have to drink anything."

Some hall people are quiet, others less so. At least once a week we get a screamer, but more commonly it is the equipment accompanying the patient that makes all the racket. Usually their IV pump starts beeping. These pumps are a marvel of high-tech design, with batteries that last about forty seconds and a power plug that is never long enough.

Since that spoilsport of hospital administrators—the JCAHO—frowns on extension cords, you end up with patients clustered around outlets.

In every department I have worked in, these clusters tend to be on the right side of the hall. Having never been in a British hospital, I wonder if their hall people wait on the left?

At Bethesda Naval Hospital we had hall people, but we didn't call them that because we had no halls. An interesting idiosyncrasy of the Navy is the use of shipboard terminology on land.

Ships don't have rooms connected by halls; they have compartments connected by passageways, and therefore so do Naval buildings. Waiting patients might have been "passageway personnel" or "temporarily delayed transient patients." Being inconvenient, these phrases would be replaced by user-friendly military acronyms such as PASWAPERS or TEMDE-TRANSPATS.

Anyone unfamiliar with these terms would be referred to the NAVDI-CAC, the *Naval Dictionary of Acronyms*.

We have a lot of hall people who seem to spend days out there. Ambulance drivers can be thanked for much of this. Ambulance drivers are very busy people—they wait for no one, not even a patient who needs a two-minute chest film.

If they don't have to rush out and pick someone up they just rush out and drive around. Two hours later they rush back to pick up your patient and rush her back to the nursing home from whence she came.

I usually try to say "hi" to all our hall people and occasionally they want to chat. Some days I may have the same conversation three or four times with one patient in the hall. The patient doesn't mind because he has Alzheimer's. I don't mind because I don't remember.

We're building a new hospital and the architects tell me it is designed with special holding areas for stretchers and wheelchair-bound patients to eliminate the hall people. It won't work. Hall people are like living expenses—they will always increase to a level just beyond your capacity to handle them.

Farewell to Tech Appreciation Week

Every November we celebrate National Radiologic Technology Week. It used to be called "Technologist Appreciation Week," and since I tend to live in the past that's what I call it. I believe the time has come to do away with both of these misnomers.

From my perspective, the relationship between radiologists and technologists is complex. Most of the techs in my department see it in simpler terms: They do the real work and we make the real money.

Unfortunately, such discussions usually come up after three of them have wrestled thirty minutes with a screaming four-year-old to get three views of a normal foot. They know the foot is normal before the film is processed because the kid has been kicking them the whole time. I then spend about four minutes reviewing and dictating the case. Who did the most work?

I know the technologists I work with appreciate the difference in our training. They realize a radiologist's training takes longer and is more comprehensive. How society decides whom and what to reward is beyond my grasp.

Is a movie star really worth more per year than the budget of some hospitals? I doubt that any patient cares about Madonna or Michael Jordan when they come in for a barium enema or a lung biopsy, but they do know the importance of a pleasant, efficient, well-trained technologist at that moment. Naturally, I like to think I earn my salary, but I believe most technologists deserve more than they get.

We try to partially compensate for this in several ways. Making a big deal out of this week is one. All celebrations in our department center around food, but we go all-out during this week. Our group buys breakfast and lunch one day, the hospital buys it another day, and we hit up the various drug and film people for other meals. In sum, we put out about two million calories of appreciation.

There is also a hospital-sponsored awards dinner. We all get together with our families to recognize those techs who have gone the extra mile.

Of course, here again it is done with the maximum possible effect on our blood cholesterol.

All this tasty appreciation is nice, but in the long run; the ongoing relationship between physicians and technologists is a more important determinant of department morale and job satisfaction. How does one evaluate this relationship?

If your technologist pulls a gun on you, things may not be good.

If your office is filled with black balloons when you come to work, and it isn't your birthday, look behind you.

Do you find yourself getting lots of paper cuts because someone is sharpening the edges of the film jackets?

Do your technologists point out your errors?

Radiology is a science/art based on perception. You can only diagnose what you see. You may be reading black when the pathology is white. Your frontal lobe may still be trying to figure out why the car wouldn't start that morning. Whatever the reason, you will not discern all the findings on every film. If you don't see it, you can't interpret it; you can't even waffle over it and show it to your partners. How do you minimize this danger?

Presumably, in a teaching hospital at least two physicians see every exam. Those of us in other settings don't have that luxury. But at least one technologist sees every exam. That tech usually has years of experience looking at studies. On any given exam, the tech may be concentrating on the white when your rods and cones are stuck on black. Does the tech point out your errors or step back and let you bury yourself?

I like to review most exams with the tech present. I'll frequently ask, "Have I missed anything?" "Do you see something else?" or just "What do you think?" If I don't ask and the tech has a question, he or she asks. Of course it is rare that a tech bails me out, and then I may not admit it ("Good, I wanted to see if you were paying attention"), but we both know that the patient and I are better off.

So let's get rid of "Appreciation Week." Appreciate your techs all year long. Use them to their full potential. This year we need to be honest with ourselves and celebrate Feed-a-Tech Week.

Chicago or Bust! Eleven Reasons
To Be There

Having established myself as the Paul and Juhl of rural radiology, I am constantly besieged with pesky questions about the annual RSNA meeting.

It is two weeks before the RSNA meeting and I just found out I can go. Any recommendations on where I can stay? The Hilton Hotel—in Detroit. You can't get any closer than that after October unless you want to sleep in a subway station.

I'm from the South and I'm afraid I will freeze to death if I go to Chicago in the winter. That is not a question, just a lame excuse for not attending. I, too, come from the genteel side of the War of Northern Aggression, and I have survived several trips to the tundra. Just bring all the clothes you own, and don't go outside.

Why are the name tags at the RSNA meeting different colors? This allows sales personnel to quickly determine who is worth talking to. In the past a blue tag indicated a physician member of the Society, someone with direct influence on purchases of imaging equipment. In the new-and-improved healthcare system, a blue tag probably won't get you the time of day on the commercial exhibit floor.

Are the people with the little oak leaf stuck to their name tags dangerous? No, they are the good guys. They realize their prosperity is due in large part to the generally high professional status of radiology. They are giving back to the field in at least a small way, by supporting the RSNA research and education fund. The radiologists to avoid are the ones without the leaf.

Why do the education and research grants always seem to go to really esoteric topics? Because all the easy descriptive things have been done. Look at your journals: ninety percent of the articles appeal to one percent of the radiologists. Of course, twenty-five years ago Dr. Hounsfield had trouble financing his "esoteric" project, and it sent your kids through college.

What are the yellow cars you see all over the streets and lined up at hotels in Chicago? I believe they are called taxicabs. Last year in my *Advisor* column I made a joke about waiting for the buses provided by the RSNA. A world-famous California radiologist wrote and told me (among other things) about the existence of taxis, which, according to him, I could take with no wait. He also told me that "radiology is not a game." Thank you.

How do I get my name on one of those multiauthor scientific exhibits or journal articles? This is difficult. You must actually walk through the room where the research is being done or the article is being written.

I am into computers. Will I enjoy the RSNA meeting? You will be in absolute ecstasy. The only things there not linked to computers are the toilets. You will particularly like infoRad. A few years ago, attending infoRad was like walking into a "Far Side" cartoon about computer nerds, but each year it becomes more user-friendly. Now, even general nerds like me can get a lot of useful information from the exhibits. Don't miss it.

Does everyone in Japan have gastric cancer and a liver tumor? Judging from the scientific exhibits and the radiology literature, I believe so.

Is there anything to do at night at the RSNA? Dumb question. The meeting stays open well into the evening; of course, by 5:00 P.M., I'm usually brain dead. Besides, there are more good restaurants and fancy malls in Chicago than you can shake a stick at. You also need to let your equipment suppliers know you will be at the meeting, since they put on the really good after-hours programs. Some are held in galleries and museums, but I can't tell you how to get invited to them. Of course, if you're a small-town guy like me, even the large movie theaters with excellent sound systems are good for a cheap thrill.

How long should I stay in Chicago? I don't know. Three days seems inadequate, and all week is exhausting. If someone else is paying, stay as long as you can.

Why does the meeting always start on Thanksgiving weekend? The organizers of our annual meeting do not like spending holidays with their families, and they have a low tolerance for leftover turkey.

Riding the Roller Coaster of Diagnostic Certainty

Like the kV on an old generator, my self-confidence seems to wax and wane. Sometimes the reason is obvious, while at other times it is as clear as an ultrasound of a 400-pound abdomen.

Attending a good CME course is one obvious confidence-builder. Last spring I attended a radiology review course sponsored by the University of Florida. This was one of those courses given right before the anal boards (as opposed to the written boards) to capitalize on the paranoia of senior residents. The course covers almost every topic in general radiology in six days. You can miss an entire organ system if you go to the rest room at the wrong time.

I sat next to a nice guy from the Midwest who was there for the same reason as I was: It had been a while since our residencies and we wanted to brush up on our general knowledge. We were surrounded by current residents, who seemed very sharp. It reminded me how much smarter I felt right after I finished my boards than I do now.

Show me a film back then and I could fire off a list of five or ten differentials in a heartbeat. The lists come much slower now, but then none of my referring physicians wants to hear a list of ten possibilities. In my hospital, four is about max, and if I can't narrow it down to one or two I have to listen to a string of old jokes about hedges. Still, back when I could fire off those lists I felt very confident, so it was nice to relearn a lot of that information.

There are other events that have an immediate effect on my confidence-meter. Making a really good diagnosis, particularly an uncommon one, is always satisfying. Finding a small lesion on a plain film and confirming its presence by CT and/or pathology is also encouraging. Finding a medium-sized lesion with an old image of a small lesion in the film jacket (clearly visible in retrospect) will ruin any day. Of course some of the factors affecting one's intelligence on a daily basis are less apparent.

The one I find most intriguing is whose office I am standing in at the time my mouth starts moving. I am always smarter and more definitive in someone else's office.

"No, Jim, I wouldn't worry about those microcalcifications. There are only four of them and they have a pretty benign morphology."

On my own viewbox, such a mammogram might induce seizures.

The process is not limited to mammography. SPECT thallium studies, the ultimate test of one's imagination, are much easier to read over someone's shoulder. Lung scans also become a breeze using a combination of the Biello system and someone else's viewbox.

This phenomenon of inflated confidence is intriguing. For me, it seems to be a function of whose name will be at the bottom of the report. Like those mindless advice-givers in almost every newspaper and magazine, it is easy to know just what to do, if someone else has to do it.

A similar process is often apparent in lecture halls. The confidence of some speakers is both inspiring and unbelievable. "Obviously" this and "clearly" that, they have a definitive answer for every complex case. It sometimes seems as if they're using different film than our department. I have been tempted to ask who sells this film with no gray areas. Of course, on the rare occasion that I give a talk, I too become a fountain of decisiveness and diagnostic pearls.

During my residency, we had a regular conference wherein residents presented cases and taught their fellow serfs. People became very authoritative when they were the "instructor." Given the dubious source of the diagnostic gems, some of us called it the "black pearl" conference.

This roller-coaster ride of self-confidence is difficult for one's ego. It is also unavoidable, since there are only two alternatives. I have known radiologists with little or no confidence; their reports are long and descriptive with no helpful conclusion for the referring physician. The other extreme, the doctor who thinks he or she is always right, is obnoxious. So I try to enjoy the peaks and tolerate the valleys. And, as on a real roller coaster, screaming profanities during times of rapid descent can be helpful.

1995

Beware the Invasion of the Vending Machines

Last summer, the vice president of the hospital where I was practicing brought me an interesting piece of mail. It was a slick, thirty-one-page "expression of interest" from a group I'll call Greedy Doctor Imaging. This group is "ready and able to provide high-quality yet cost-efficient professional radiology services to your facility at a level of efficient delivery unparalleled by your present vendor."

I had never thought of myself as a "present vendor." I am a physician, a father, a spouse, writer of sorts and a lousy singer, but not a present vendor.

And what is "efficient delivery" in radiology? Does that mean you can perform a barium enema twice as fast? Your patients may not appreciate such efficiency. "Efficient" is a buzzword for administrators and insurance folks; compassionate is the word preferred by physicians and patients.

Greedy Doctor Imaging's president and radiologist-in-chief is the chair of radiology at two hospitals, and holds an academic appointment at a major East Coast university. Does that mean he is a "present vendor" at these institutions?

No doubt he is an excellent radiologist. The brochure describes him and his associates as "experienced," "adaptable," "expert," "highly skilled," "seasoned," "highly talented," and "accomplished." And this was only the first page. On the second, they are "renowned," "fine board-certified," "board eligible" and "well-groomed." Well, if there's one thing I can't bear, it's an unkempt radiologist.

They also must look good in smocks, since they all "will wear laundered, well-fitting and fresh professional smocks." I personally prefer a scrub shirt and trousers, but I admit I have never seen myself in a smock—or a skirt and blouse for that matter.

Greedy Medical Imaging's executive committee includes other elite East Coast radiologists and a renowned nuclear medicine physician from the Midwest. The committee will supervise "on-site" radiologists. These radi-

47

ologists are not specified, but they will be "delightful." Patients' interactions with them will be "delightful." Even their dealings with insurance companies will be "delightful." Snow White, M.D. at your service!

You might ask yourself why these stellar radiologists want to take over radiology at my 125-bed rural hospital (no mistake, they specified it by name more than fifteen times). I found the answer, oozing sincerity, in their proposal: "With a strong belief that our business activities should produce a public benefit in addition to benefiting the corporation, Greedy Doctor Imaging selects undertakings that provide opportunities to truly contribute." Among their contributions, of course, would be my future unemployment.

When I learned that a group of well-credentialed radiologists wants to "contribute" in my little hospital hours from their homes, I was puzzled. Don't their own institutions pay them? Is fresh air so hard to find? Or do they just want more money?

The unsolicited expression of interest is very businesslike. In my mind, doctors who treat other doctors on a business level rather than a professional level are not physicians but businessmen. This is not a bad thing to be, but it appears that one of the unfortunate goals of healthcare reform is to turn all physicians into business people. Those who are good business people are thriving, at least temporarily. The rest of us are flailing like residents doing their first BE while we wait and pray for a neatly packaged solution from the American College of Radiology. In the long run, we are counting on people coming back to doctors who are physicians first.

My hospital administrator asked me what he should do with the proposal from Greedy Doctor Imaging. I said, "Accept it. Let them take over the entire radiology department at King's Daughter Hospital next month." These shrewd businessmen sent a proposal to staff the radiology department of a hospital that closed its doors forever last September.

I now practice at a new hospital seven miles down the road, and we have plenty of radiology vendors. In the not-too-distant past, hospital administrators were the enemy. Now they are protecting me from the "vending machines."

Does MQSA Portend Changes to Come?

The Mammography Quality Standards Act is shifting into high gear. I stopped by the MQSA booth at the Radiological Society of North America meeting to ask a few questions and pick up some information. Both goals were easily accomplished; the staff was friendly and knowledgeable, and like any federal agency, the first thing it apparently did was buy a printing press.

As we all know, the American College of Radiology began its accreditation program in mammography a few years ago. While it has been somewhat of a hassle for those who were already doing a good job, it has been very effective at improving the overall quality of mammography in the United States. For many of us who thought we were doing good mammography, we learned we could do it even better. The ACR program has saved lives, at a very reasonable cost.

Like most radiologists, I sweat a disproportionate amount over mammograms. The breast is an anatomically simple organ, with a limited number of diseases affecting a few cell types. It is also an emotion-laden gland that commands a great deal of public scrutiny. Worst of all, the differences between benign and malignant lesions are often only visible through a retrospectoscope. I suspect the only thing that would bother most radiologists (who are male) more is a similar spectrum of disease and primary treatment modality affecting the pendulous urethra.

By passing the MQSA, our presumably well-intentioned Congress has created yet another bureaucratic division. The staff members I spoke with in Chicago told me that MQSA has an initial budget of $13 million for implementing the program. They still need to hire 250 to 300 more inspectors to really get the program rolling.

What I find surprising about the MQSA is the zealous approach of the program in the face of diminishing returns. The national quality of mammography is not perfect, but due to the ACR program I suspect the norm is far above other outpatient imaging modalities.

Should similar FDA standards for mammography be applied to general radiography, most of the X-ray machines in this country would be shut down. Certainly the vast majority of "spinal manipulators," who seem to have neither collimators nor mAs controls, would have to turn off their units.

If the government were to take the same leap into chest radiology, which involves multiple organs and myriad diseases, we would be trampled by inspectors.

The MQSA is not going to decrease healthcare expenditures. Besides the obvious expense of establishing a new bureaucracy, there are other, less obvious costs. Paid employees will have to generate the mountains of statistics and documentation required by the legislation. Of course, with thousands of mammography sites busy hiring additional clerical workers, and the government now paying for mammograms, one could argue that this is actually a federal jobs program.

Another hidden cost is the requirement that every physician reading mammograms complete a regular amount of CME. The up-front cost of a course is negligible and education is always a good idea. However, every time I spend a week looking at little ditzels that are subsequently shown to be malignant, I get paranoid. When I get back from such a course, the number of special views, six-month follow-ups and negative biopsies—none of which come free—go through the roof.

Of course, one could argue that the point of such courses is exactly this kind of threshold readjustment, but it still adds to the cost.

No doubt the level of mammography in the United States will improve even further with enforcement of the MQSA. Additional lives will be saved and more women will be diagnosed at an earlier stage of their disease. Should this level of disease-specific management by legislation ever be applied more broadly to radiology, the entire field would see an elevation of standards. However, the current fifteen percent of GNP spent on healthcare will look like a paltry sum, and the suicide rate among radiology administrators will rise even higher.

Ultrasound: The Point-and-Shoot Modality

Most radiologists are all too familiar with turf wars, but I wonder what nonmedical people think of when they hear the term.

Perhaps they imagine the theme from "The Twilight Zone" playing softly in the background. Then comes the voice of Rod Serling: "Picture if you will, two intelligent adults, standing in the bowels of a large modern hospital, throwing large clumps of zoysia grass at each other. To the victor go prestige, power and great financial rewards."

Compression ultrasound of the deep veins has been coveted by our vascular lab (run by vascular surgeons and cardiologists, and open 9:00 to 5:00) since we instituted it about six years ago. They want to offer the same procedure, but they won't infringe on our exclusive rights after 5:00 P.M. How thoughtful.

Obstetrical ultrasound has been unofficially divided in our area on the basis of payor classification for several years. My unbiased opinion: Those who can't pay get referred for the better study. This has a certain ironic appeal to it.

Certain areas of imaging (the ones that look easy) are particularly vulnerable to encroachment. If you ignore all the subtleties and concentrate only on whether or not there is an infiltrate, chest radiography is pretty simple. Why not just snap a few films in your office?

Ultrasound is another area that appears deceptively simple. Several years ago Dr. Roy Filly wrote one of my favorite pieces of radiology commentary, "Ultrasound, the next stethoscope, alas" (*Radiology* 1988;167:400). Filly drew an analogy between the cretins who walk around every hospital with a stethoscope displayed around their neck, unaware of the diagnostic tool's potential, and the current trend for anyone who can afford a machine and a weekend course to set up an ultrasound practice.

Urology, and the blossoming field of prostate ultrasound (we don't know if it really helps but insurers pay for it) is a prime example. Manufacturers offer weekend courses at nice resorts that virtually pay for themselves if you put one of their cheap machines in your office. Apparently, abdominal ultrasound is the next frontier.

Recently, I received a brochure for a course in Orlando entitled "Diagnostic and interventional ultrasound for surgeons." The course consists of 16.5 hours of lectures and workshops on abdominal and small parts (breast, thyroid and parathyroid) imaging and interventional procedures. Tuition is $2,495.

Maybe I am cynical, but a tuition of $2,495 seems like a neon sign flashing "LUCRATIVE." Does one go to a 16.5-hour course including porcine labs and phantom models for ultrasound-guided biopsies to communicate better with your radiologist?

Remember how good you were at ultrasound on your first rotation as a resident? By 9:00 A.M. of the third day you already had 16.5 hours of training. At that point the sonographers were still showing me how to keep from squirting gel on my clothes.

The faculty for the Orlando course included twelve physicians: nine surgeons, two Danish ultrasonographers and one American radiologist/ultrasonographer. I talked to the American radiologist. In return for being perceived as selling out his specialty, he gets a discounted trip to the Magic Kingdom and a small honorarium.

Actually, he was in a pretty tight spot. I assume he knows more ultrasound than the surgeons do. He can turn them down, and they will have the course without him. Any misinformation that he might have corrected, or any sense he might have conveyed of the limited ability one has after only 16.5 hours of training would be lost. Or he can participate in the course, knowing that the knowledge disseminated may help unknown patients, but possibly work against him (and the rest of us) financially. Fortunately, with my limited abilities, I don't have to wrestle with such invitations.

Given the current state of medicine, turf battles seem inevitable. Our best defense is to provide the highest quality service with the patient's best interest at the forefront. With that in mind, I have decided to offer the following weekend course this spring: "Appendectomies and Vasectomies for General Radiologists."

A Day in the Life of a Wet Film Reviewer

Sitting at the wet read desk reviewing a set of sinus films:

Doctor: "Which tech did these films?"

Tech: "Sherri."

Doctor: "What room is she using?"

Tech: "ER 3."

Doctor, speaking on the phone: "Sherri, are the collimators in there broken?"

Sherri: "No, the history is allergic rhinitis, so I thought you would like to check the air around the patient's head for allergens."

Do they teach these retorts in tech school? My approach is to be light-hearted when I criticize technical factors. If you're going to be heavy-handed in your criticism, you must be willing to go in the room and show the techs how to do it better. Letting them know you noticed a problem without being critical is usually all the reminding most people need to maintain their standards.

Some people will persist, however. We have at least one tech who is a follower of Darth Vader, which is to say, she worships the Dark Side. We call her The Torch.

Doctor: "This film looks dark."

Torch: "You know, I think the viewbox by the processor is brighter than yours. The film looked fine up there."

Doctor: "You think this should be repeated?"

Torch: "No. That's why God made hot-lights."

Doctor: "This may be too dark."

Torch: "I thought Dr. Sensitive Retinas (one of your partners who isn't in the room) was going to be reading it, and you know she likes them dark."

There is a solution—Halogen hot-lights. But you only have ten seconds to read the film before it melts.

Rotation on pediatric chest films is another recurrent problem. Maybe all little kids walk around slightly turned to one side and I just never noticed. Or some children may think they are having a chest X-ray because they did something wrong. My own kids won't look directly at me when they have a reason to be guilty. More likely, X-rays are bent out of shape by incessant loud screaming and the patients just look rotated.

Photo-timers seemed to get blamed for a lot of exposure problems. These much maligned devices have the following life cycle:

1) new photo-timer: needs to be calibrated

2) recently calibrated photo-timer: have to get used to it

3) drifting photo-timer: needs recalibration

4) recalibrated phototimer: have to get used to it

5) bad photo-timer: needs to be replaced

6) new photo-timer . . . .

Some of our worst films come from the emergency room at night. This is not too surprising since we get drunks, sociopaths and misfits populating our emergency room at night. And the patients can be difficult, too.

Actually, I am proud of our evening and night techs. They do a good job, considering it is usually the newest and least experienced among them who get stuck with night shifts, when there is no one around to ask for help. It's the old swim-or-sink philosophy: The tech learns to swim or the patient sinks.

Reading out the ER board in the morning, you can usually tell how it went the previous night. Multiple trauma series and numerous portable films indicate major frustration. I think sometimes the ER doctors and nurses play games with our department when their night is slow.

I often don't have to deduce what the previous night was like; I just read the notes the technologists write on the request. These vary from short clinical histories to long descriptions of uncooperative and antisocial patient behavior. I know I'm in for some entertaining narrative (and lousy films) when I see a long note ending with a string of exclamation marks. There is probably a correlative study to be done relating the number of exclamation marks to both the patient's blood alcohol level and the incidence of significant injury.

Not all areas of our department are plagued with technical problems and excuses. You never hear mammo techs blame a problem on the processor, cassettes, cleaning people, tube, generator or phase of the moon.

Don't Forget to Throw in the Barium Enema Kit

As part of radiology's yearlong centennial festivities, 3M and Radiology Centennial Inc. are preparing a time capsule. These folks want to store away representative items in a capsule to be opened in one hundred years. Since this implies the specialty of radiology will exist a century from now, I consider the people behind this plan to be serious optimists.

I see one real flaw in their proposal. It states that "Duplicates of the time capsule materials will be archived at the American College of Radiology and selected medical libraries." No way, José. As anyone familiar with time capsule decorum can tell you, once a capsule is filled, you throw away the records. Otherwise, you destroy the mystery surrounding its opening. Do you want to study a list all year of the presents you have coming Christmas morning?

It's weird to contemplate what medicine will be like in one hundred years. I suspect people may speak of exposing humans to ionizing radiation for "medical purposes" in the same way we refer to the medicinal application of leeches. We can assume the capsule openers will be familiar with the general evolution of medical imaging, so we ought to put in some surprises, and some of the more routine tools and accessories we use that may not otherwise survive.

The press releases don't mention the size of this capsule. I used to take my kids to the Smithsonian Institution every year or two to see the dinosaurs. It takes a large room to hold their remains. Adults and kids alike can be seen wandering around in awe, wondering if such cumbersome beasts really did exist. We could go for the same effect in radiology. Is there room in the time capsule for a PET scanner?

The capsule collection should also have a barium enema kit along with the instructions for patient prep. Our descendants will never believe we actually did this to patients. I suspect they will be just as incredulous that any patient would even consider going through the necessary preparation.

Of course, some of my patients just ignore the prep anyway, and assume I won't notice when I do the test.

We want the contents of the capsule to be evaluated in an appropriate context. There needs to be a collection of current literature from other medical fields, such as family practice, surgery, reflexology, chiropractic medicine, homeopathic medicine and the *National Enquirer*. That way we can be seen as a point on a continuum, rather than as a fringe group.

My life would be nicer if I could ship off a few ER physicians for one hundred years. It is amazing how my sleep pattern is affected by which doctor is covering the ER at my hospital.

The people who come up with the prices for software upgrades on MRI machines could also be sent packing. By then, inflation should make their prices seem fairly reasonable.

There are a few things I can honestly suggest for the time capsule. Hitachi and Radiographics have put many of the RSNA scientific exhibits on compact disk. These exhibits are my favorite part of the annual Chicago chaos, so I think these CDs are terrific, although I wish they "talked." The CDs should be expanded to include all the exhibits, and not just the good ones. Part of the fun of the exhibits is seeing how far past the left field fence some people have taken "radiology."

For the last five years I have been using a compression device in fluoro called an F spoon, which ought to be included. While I am amazed that a piece of molded plastic can cost seventy-five dollars, I have to admit it is worth the money. It is the kind of thing you look at and say, "Now why didn't I think of that?" And then you imagine all the money you could have made if you had thought of it. Which starts you trying to come up with some equally novel creation to generate your own easy money. Unfortunately, those ideas are not as simple to generate as they look. So then you go back to reading that stack of films.

If there is any room available after all the above is included, my department (and probably a lot of others around the country) would be willing to part with some of the low-level radioactive waste we are holding. In one hundred years, the contaminated materials will be safe, and probably just as exciting to review as some of the other things likely to be found in the capsule.

Radiology Batting Averages on Parade

My daughter has recently become interested in collecting baseball cards. It's a fun hobby for her, and I've learned a few things too. For example, the value of the cards rise and fall unpredictably, a little like Medicare payments and the RBRVS.

You can spot real collectors by their knowledge of the statistics printed on the back of the cards. A player's record is there for everyone to read and memorize.

We have similar statistics in medicine, but they're known as QA (quality assurance). Another important difference between medicine and baseball relates to averages. A baseball player who hits .400 is a phenomenon, whereas .400 isn't the goal of most radiologists, unless they happen to practice in the field of mammography.

It seems to me that the logical progression of the National Practitioner Data Bank is the development of "doctor cards." Imagine yourself striking a pose with an ultrasound transducer or angio catheter proudly displayed. Or perhaps you could be pensively studying a film hung upside down on the viewbox, like those seen in many medical advertisements. Radiologists who like to flatter themselves by billing their film-reading panels as "stump the stars" could develop special all-star limited editions. Researchers at the National Institutes of Health could write the copy for the flip side of the cards, thereby giving us all good-looking statistics.

Not many of us would want our batting averages widely circulated, for good reason. Medicine in general, and doctors in particular, do not handle mistakes well. I'm embarrassed by mine, and I don't like the thought of letting down a patient entrusted to my care. United States medical education seems to foster such feelings, even though we know we learn best from our mistakes. I don't remember too much praise or analysis of my errors when I was rotating through surgery, but then I was working for people who knew they were perfect.

For many years my group has correlated its readings with the pathologic diagnosis. It is a simple system. I get a copy of every pathology report and I identify those that might have a related imaging study. Our file room pulls the jacket if there has been a recent exam, and I match our findings with the path report. Each case is then reviewed by every radiologist in the group.

Clearly this is a biased sampling, but there is still much to be learned from the exercise. The most obvious discovery is that Americans are being whittled away. For every major pathology report, there are reams of reports describing little skin lumps and bumps that have been excised.

You also get to see your own runs, hits and errors. Everyone else in the group gets to see them too. It can be fun to review a case on which a very subtle finding was used to make the diagnosis. Conversely, you feel stupid when an obvious finding is not correctly interpreted. More importantly, you realize that we all make mistakes, and the best way to learn from them is to review them in a nonjudgmental way (e.g., "Brad, what were you smoking when you missed that big thing?").

Our group has debated whether such a detailed record of our work could ever come back to haunt us. So far we believe that the pros far outweigh the cons . . . but then Richard Nixon thought his secret tapes were a good idea, too.

A bigger problem with "batting average" publicity is the inherent bias in the data. For the most part, the Data Bankers only want to record your errors. A more important number, but nearly impossible to quantify, is how much good you do your patients. How much credence do referring physicians put in a report with your name at the bottom?

If such biased numbers are made public, will patients use them to choose their doctors? Laypeople I talk to generally want a physician who is compassionate—a friendly, caring person who will listen to them, spend time with them and treat them as an equal. Even though "to err is human," I don't hear many people saying they'd easily forgive a doctor who made a mistake on them.

Ups and Downs of Small-Town Radiology

I live in a small town, and until recently, I worked in a small hospital across the street from my house. In the last year our hospital merged with another nearby community hospital. The two original facilities were closed and a new medical center was built halfway between the two towns. Now I commute to work (eight miles) by car or bicycle. In the past, I could be called in to do an emergency IVP at night and have the study completed before I had completely awakened. Now I wake up on the way in, which means my late night personality has improved, but my interpretations haven't.

One of the major differences I noticed when I moved to a rural practice was the loss of anonymity. In a metropolitan hospital I was one of "the radiologists." Outside of my own circle of friends, few people associated my name or face with healthcare in the community. Immediately after coming to our small town I was recognized in stores as "that new doctor." At a local fair, a man I didn't know introduced me to a number of people as "the doctor who found the peanut his son choked on." Radiologists are often referred to as doctors' doctors, but I find it nice to be a people's doctor too. Full-time mammographers probably have the same experience.

Being recognized is not always fun. Imagine being introduced to a woman who greets you with "You're the guy who misdiagnosed my breast cancer." It was very uncomfortable and embarrassing until I figured out that my error was recommending a six-month follow-up of a 3-mm lesion on a screening mammo. She subsequently had a Stage 1 cancer removed and I feel good about my pickup, although half the town has probably heard about my "error." If only all my mistakes were like that one.

Shortly after I moved to Staunton, our hospital switched from xeromammography to screen-film mammography. There is no question that one can see more on screen-film images. There is also no doubt that screen-film studies require greater breast compression; which many of the women parishioners at my church mention to me each Sunday.

The administration of our new medical center demanded a merger of the hospital-based physician groups from the two smaller hospitals. That, plus the addition of a neuroradiologist and an angio-interventionalist, took me from a three-person to an eight-person group in a short time. While three people can easily agree on many things, eight will seldom agree on anything. We had the adjustment problems one might expect from a shotgun wedding, without the fun that usually precedes it.

Small-hospital medicine can also be confusing in terms of protocol. Many of the technologists I work with are my friends outside the hospital. At work they refer to me as Dr. Tipler. What are they supposed to call me in social settings? A title should be used to convey relevant information. In the hospital it is important that patients understand quickly who I am and why we are meeting. At a party it really doesn't matter.

The best part about a small-town practice is your relationship with referring physicians. Most of them are not into ego games. If you show that you can help them take care of their patients, they will make you a part of the team.

Our new hospital is designed for efficient use of the radiologists' time. We have separate work areas where studies can be brought to us by the technologists working in the surrounding rooms. While this is efficient, a lot of informal exchanges of information have been sacrificed. Clinicians have to make a conscious effort to find me, which they seldom choose to do. Now I rely on the detailed clinical information provided on the request, histories like "pain" or "fever."

I hear that urban jobs are becoming harder to find. Radiology residents should take a long look at working in community practice. True, it can be frustrating keeping up with all areas of radiology, but the rewards are great. Unfortunately, you can't get away from all the urban problems. Last week we had a city-wide crime wave—one bike and three lawn mowers were stolen.

Learning to Jump Through Hoops

The medical staff in my rural hospital is in an uproar; modern medicine is pounding on our door, demanding changes. This is not to imply that our tools or techniques are out of date, just that we are used to getting paid for our work.

Our county's largest employer is a plant that makes synthetic fibers used in all those skintight exercise clothes you see on people who are not exercising, and obviously never do. The home office (out of state) has mandated "managed care" for all employees by 1996, and they have contracted with "PHLEGMA," a large healthcare corporation, to arrange these services. Now my group, and all the other physicians in the area, are faced with our first Managed Care Agreement.

PHLEGMA is using a very aggressive approach in the contract negotiations. The fact that healthcare costs in our county are already below the state and national averages is irrelevant. This company knows you can bleed anemic people, just not as much.

The home office and PHLEGMA think their aggressive behavior is just part of a good day's work. They have no feelings (good or bad) for me or my patients. The quality of my work is of minor concern. They want my money, and I would like to hold my losses to a minimum. I feel like a person trying to make it through a mugging.

The Managed Care Agreement is somewhat ironic. The first sentence establishes that my physician group will be referred to as "group," while PHLEGMA will be called "HealthCare." Like so many bureaucrats and administrators, PHLEGMA confuses what it is doing with providing a service.

Not all of us have our heads buried in the sand, however. Some of our medical staff have been trying for the last year to form a PHO (physician-hospital organization). Of course, now that we are actually faced with a business that wants to negotiate, interest in a PHO or some other form of coalition has skyrocketed. We have many new committees and more meetings—two surefire ways to accomplish nothing.

Our last meeting featured a consultant hired to help us form our PHO. This guy used to work for PHLEGMA and seemed very knowledgeable about its contracts and methods of operation. We've hired a former mugger to help us stay alive. We also heard from our hospital attorney, who's like our mom. He has to come with us to important meetings to tell us what we can and cannot do, without helping us to do it.

As questions were asked by the medical staff, several things became clear:

A) This game is being played with a stacked deck. Our antiquated antitrust laws are appropriately named. Large corporations can do whatever they want, and physicians can't trust anyone. We can't even talk about these things at lunch.

B) "Risk sharing" is the buzzword. If doctors will share the financial risks, they will share more of the financial gain. I don't hear a lot of talk about sharing the professional risks. On the contrary, payors are demanding to participate in care, but refusing responsibility. The old, "Well, if she gets pregnant, it's her problem" mentality.

Dealing with an organization like PHLEGMA is like talking to a military recruiter or an insurance shyster. You may be told all sorts of things, but if it isn't in writing, only you will remember it.

Some primary-care physicians are reveling in the power of the gatekeeper role. Corporate and political decision-makers think these front-line guardians are the ultimate solution. Many fail to realize that with a tool like MRI, you need a gatekeeper who knows how the gate and the tools behind it work.

It would be much simpler, and probably save even more money, if the whole process of healthcare reform/managed care were reduced to its basic core. Outside every hospital or healthcare facility, you place a course of one hundred hoops. Anytime a doctor or patient wants service, they have to run the course, and then give ten percent of their money to PHLEGMA.

Are You Allergic to Fried Chicken?

Intravenous contrast is an integral part of a general radiology practice, along with nurses who think that a three-hour wait in the ER is fine, but a ten-minute wait in radiology is a capital offense.

When I trained it seemed like everyone who had an IVP threw up. Of course, we gave them 120 cc of ionic contrast through a large bore needle as fast as we could push it. Their chemo receptors went ballistic. Now, thanks to lawyers and pharmaceutical companies, giving contrast has become more complex.

We have elaborate informed consent forms for IV contrast and our technologists question the patients directly. "Do you have any allergies?" seems like a simple question, but we get some interesting answers.

"Not that I know of." What does this mean? It isn't yes and it isn't no. It reminds me of the Watergate hearings. People were always prefacing their answers with "To the best of my recollection . . . " Of course, most of the people testifying were lawyers.

"I think so, but I don't remember what." A very helpful answer.

"Yes, those little yellow pills with the little symbol on them." Even more helpful.

The patients aren't the only ones who make it difficult, however. In spite of all the information that says the answer is irrelevant, some of our staff still insist on asking patients if they eat seafood. Then, when they get a patient who doesn't eat seafood they're in a quandary about whether to administer contrast. I like to ask if patients eat fried chicken. Everyone in the South eats fried chicken.

Nonionic contrast created a number of problems when it was introduced, and they all boiled down to money. Initially, my partners and I took the ACR's guidelines and established them as our department protocol for the use of nonionics.

We soon realized what a good thing we had on our hands. The incidence of major reactions has always been small, and that it became even smaller made life that much easier. But the big effect was on the minor reactions.

The literature always mentions the decrease in minor reactions in a perfunctory manner. The healthcare system and the hospital are willing to accept these minor inconveniences given the savings realized by using ionic contrast. That is because the administrators don't have to tighten their sphincter and rush down the hall when their technologist comes in to say, "I think the patient is having some kind of reaction."

Contrast reactions, even "minor" ones, are stressful situations because initially no one knows what is going to happen. Prior to the exam, the patient has been informed in excessive detail of all the terrible things that may happen following contrast administration. Of course, the patient thinks the worst one is happening to him.

I have to stop what I am doing, rush to the patient and quickly try to determine what is happening. The first big challenge is trying to find a stethoscope and blood-pressure cuff. We solved this problem by putting a set in every room and marking the location with a big red dot.

Then comes the medical part. Checking the ABCs, getting some vital signs and trying to calmly reassure the patient that you are in control and that he is not going to die. Treating the reaction is usually straightforward, and just about every one responds quickly. But it still takes time—my time, the technologist's time and the patient's time. It doesn't use a single administrator's time, so the stress and inconvenience are minor compared to the savings.

Another interesting thing happened soon after we started using nonionic contrast. My partners and I began to expand the selection parameters to include our families, friends and coworkers on the list of those who received nonionics. Eventually our administration allowed us to go strictly nonionic. In hospitals that still use nonionics selectively, I wonder which contrast is selected when a radiologist, a technologist or one of their spouses has an exam?

Improved contrast media are here to stay. In fact, they're multiplying like rabbits. I am a little surprised that with all this "competition," the price for these agents remains remarkably high, and remarkably similar. It must be a coincidence.

Next on Tonight Show:
Dr. R and The Rays

A century ago Dr. Roentgen was toiling away in his laboratory with an evacuated tube when he observed a glowing fluorescent screen across the room. He holed up in his lab for seven weeks and figured out most of the basic properties of the rays he had discovered. Then he shared his discovery with the world in his now classic paper.

Sometime before Roentgen's discovery, Dr. Crooke (of Crooke's tube fame) was conducting similar experiments in his lab. Around the same time he received two batches of "bad" photographic plates, which he promptly returned to the manufacturer. Only after Dr. R.'s announcement did he make the connection between his experiments and the fogged plates.

It is interesting to speculate what would happen if Dr. R. made such a monumental achievement today. Hiding away in your lab for weeks on end before sharing your discovery with the world does not sound like a modern scenario.

Being academically oriented, today's Dr. R. would probably be working in a university lab. As soon as he tried to seal his lab and work on his discovery alone, his graduate students would take notice. Soon there would be leaks to the media and he would be deluged with questions. Before any official announcement of the discovery was made, there would be many long discussions with the patent attorneys. Who owns the patent, Dr. R. or the university?

The article announcing the discovery would follow. Everyone and their brother would want their name on this one. The list of authors would be longer than the paper. Who gets to be senior author? The chairman of the department, the university president or Dr. R.?

With these questions out of the way, Dr. R. could begin the really serious work, finding venture capital to finance a start-up company for manufacturing X-ray equipment. This is only a temporary problem, since he'll very quickly be absorbed by some large conglomerate, allowing him to bail out with a platinum parachute.

The cigarette manufacturers would no doubt go into a feeding frenzy trying to buy his corporation, and thereby control X-rays. If they seized control of The Rays, chest radiography would be in serious trouble.

"Our research has shown that the lungs are very sensitive to radiation. We cannot in good conscience allow our X-ray machines to be used to look for lung disease," their pronouncement would read.

Dr. and Mrs. R. would become celebrities. "20/20" and "60 Minutes" would try to get them, but Barbara Walters would end up interviewing them in their modest living room. The doctor would be on "The Tonight Show" cracking jokes about his research. Mrs. R. could appear on "Oprah" to talk about the effects of radiation on their sex life, although radiation and romance with your spouse are rather tame material for today's talk shows.

What about Dr. Crooke and all the other researchers who unknowingly produced X-rays in their labs without making the critical observation? Perhaps Dr. Crooke would steal a page from MRI history and publish a book about himself, so everyone would know he was the real hero.

Naturally, Dr. R. would save his really big splash for our annual information orgy in Chicago. He would build a multilevel display booth the size of an aircraft carrier and import an army of equipment representatives and marketing specialists to staff the behemoth. Each night there would be a reception featuring shrimp the size of your forearm, since boiled crustaceans have become a sort of corporate reception sex symbol.

What would Dr. R. do after X-rays were assimilated into modern culture, accepted as a basic right in the U.S. and he had packed away millions? He could start a third political party and run for president, or opt for a lucrative career endorsing insurance plans. But, maybe he would just set up a free radiology clinic in an underserved area, and keep up the good work. When faced with a choice between greed and service, I hope that, like Roentgen, I would pick the latter, but I wonder how often I have missed a profound, simple observation while I was whining about fogged films.

Christmas Gifts We Can Only Dream About

Perhaps you've been wondering what to buy the people you work with for Christmas. This year some very useful but little-known products were introduced at the RSNA meeting. Let me tell you about some of them.

Technologists are going to love the new digital crest finder (DCF) from Wide-load X-ray Products. This hand-held electronic wonder is patterned after stud finders that carpenters use to find the two-by-fours inside the walls of your house. Simply select one of ten preprogrammed bony landmarks ranging from the ASIS to C7. Then slowly wave the device over the patient until the indicator dial says you are over the part selected.

"I used to dread it when a 350-pound patient climbed onto my X-ray table for a KUB. Trying to find the crest was like swimming in a bowl of pudding. My first film might end up with half the femurs or half the lungs on it. Now I just wave the DCF over the patient and find all my bony landmarks effortlessly. It's so easy that even our chief radiologist could do it," said technologist Dreama Darnell, one of the creators of the DCF.

Physicians and technologists will appreciate the new "Pain-O-Meter" developed as a joint project by NASA and the Acme Root Canal Company. Some patients scream bloody murder over a hangnail while others just grimace when you inadvertently reposition their compound fracture. Whom you believe is often a function of how you feel at the time. This can be a particular problem for technologists dealing with a screaming patient who doesn't want to move and a screaming radiologist who thinks every film must be positioned perfectly.

Now, with a Pain-O-Meter mounted on the wall, an objective digital readout is flashed every time the patient makes a sound. Ranging from "ignore this turkey" to "don't let this happen to you," the readout is constantly updated as the exam proceeds.

Ciao has always produced good ultrasound machines at very reasonable prices. The company's latest innovation may be the one that helps them take over the number-one spot. The Ciao Ovarian Magnet can be added to both transvaginal and surface transducers, and makes a great gift for your favorite sonographer. Once the transducer is in contact with the patient, you simply select either "left ovary" or "right ovary" and the ovary is immediately drawn to the scan head. Scanning times are dramatically reduced and so is patient discomfort. The only problems have been when the button is accidentally pushed during a gallbladder or thyroid study.

Just about every hospital in the country has a Pigg-O-Stat pediatric positioner. Their new Serenity model may be just the gift for someone in your department. Now the child is not only immobilized, but also sealed in a radiolucent soundproof chamber. The Serenity Deluxe model may prove even more popular—it has room to put both parents in the chamber with the child.

Angiographers worldwide would love to find a bottle of Artery Seal under their tree. Inventor/ interventionalist Dr. Rabid Tempkin modeled his product after the radiator sealant car mechanics have used for years.

"I never really liked holding the groin after a study, especially if the patient was heparinized," Tempkin said. "For years I have made my techs hold, but now when I get ready to pull out I just squirt in a glob of Artery Seal and we all take a long lunch."

Florida Nuclear Products introduced its new line of Clarity Filters for nuclear medicine computers. Nuclear medicine guru and CEO W. Dew Rain designed these filters with the general radiologist in mind. He noticed a certain disdain among radiologists for the lack of anatomic detail and edge sharpness in most nuclear images. Based on fuzzy logic, these filters "creatively enhance" the image to a level of sharpness formerly found only in nuclear medicine texts. Now every lung scan will look like it was lifted from Mettler, and cardiac images will actually resemble the heart.

Those who didn't make it to the meeting will just have to hope at least one of these items shows up under their Christmas tree.

1996

Networking at the Mother of All Networks

I love the annual RSNA meeting in Chicago because of its size and scope—you can learn something about any topic in radiology that interests you. Each year there are certain hot topics that seem to dominate the event. Last year, spiral CT was the "innovation de jour," while this year PACS and "network" were the major buzzwords.

"Network" is one of those words that has taken on a new meaning in modern America, like "gay" and "rap." I still think of network as a noun, although more people are using it as a verb. Do you and I need a network in place to network? If I ask you how to get on a network, have we just networked and thereby created a new network? How many networkers does it take to form a network?

In Chicago this year, both the verb and the noun were popular. You could buy any kind of electronic imaging network imaginable, and radiologists networking with one another will supposedly yield a quantum leap in the quality of medical care.

I personally do not know many radiologists or hospitals using PACS in a significant way, but the manufacturers seem to be using the Field of Dreams approach popularized by Kevin Costner—build it and they will come. Every other booth in the Technical Exhibits Hall (a.k.a., trade show) was a company selling PACS equipment or software. All the major vendors devoted lots of space to their own imaging network divisions or services. Obviously, the vendors believe there's gold in them thar hills.

InfoRad (the electronic component of the scientific exhibits) featured an elaborate Disney-style show and display entitled "The Radiology Department of The Future." The display's major focus was the effect that PACS and communications networks will have on our future. Interestingly, the radiology department of the future was strongly influenced by military medicine, a major funder of PACS research. When I was in the Navy ten years ago, the system was short on basics like doctors and support personnel, but heavy on administrators and administrative nurses. Looking around my own hospital today, I've decided that the military can predict the future.

While networks of equipment don't bother me, people getting together to network do. I have been dealing with TV networks since my childhood, so tying together computers or imaging equipment to exchange information seems appropriate. But people in medicine exchange more than hard data when they interact, and I would rather know someone than network with them. However, my favorite network on TV now is the Weather Channel, so a lot of people would probably rather network with me than get to know me.

Radiologist networks are already appearing. A network of five major teaching departments in the Northeast was offering its teleconsulting services to private radiologists at the RSNA meeting this year. When I asked whether it would contract directly with a hospital to provide radiology services, the network's representatives said, "Only if the hospital contacted us first; we are not marketing our services to them at this time." I guess the goal is to give their residents a lot of experience in their training institution, because there will be so little work being done elsewhere.

Another network of sorts that has intrigued me for years is one I've noticed chiefly at the RSNA meeting. I think of this network as organized radiology, somewhat analogous to organized medicine and organized religion. While it obviously does a lot for our specialty, organized radiology is not without its quirks.

Next time you go to RSNA, notice all the radiologists with ribbons on their name badges. Do these ribbons serve a function? In an emergency, should I find someone with a red or white ribbon hanging on his badge? Does a blue ribbon get you a free lunch? Can I ask anyone with a "presenter" ribbon a question about bone scintigraphy or gated SPECT or is the name of the presenter important, too? Why do these ribbons remind me of the ubiquitous "My child is an honor student at Podunk Elementary" bumper stickers? I'm not sure, but next year I'm taking a bunch of ribbons with me to the RSNA meeting to find out.

Fond Memories of Mentors Past

I have a certain fondness for uroradiology. The field centers around a well-defined organ system, which makes it manageable but still challenging. You also interact a lot with urologists, who generally are more laid-back surgical types. The same cannot be said about a field like neuroradiology.

But the real reason for my attraction is probably the influence of several key mentors in my radiology career. We tend to underestimate the role such figures play in our lives. I think it is because people who care about you, who want you to grow and know you need to be challenged, may not make your life easier at the time. Only in retrospect do you realize that teachers you thought were okay were actually great, and the ones you thought were jerks were really very good. Of course, some teachers still seem like turkeys in retrospect.

By the beginning of my senior year in medical school I knew I was going into family practice. I interviewed at family practice residencies all over the East Coast. Since I was on a Navy scholarship, I concentrated on Navy programs.

Near the end of my senior year I took an elective in radiology and saw the light in the darkness. Here were people having fun, figuring out the most intriguing medical problems on a daily basis. The field was a combination of Sherlock Holmes, general medicine and *Star Wars*. At the last minute, I applied for and won one of the great mistakes of modern medicine, the radiology internship. The main redeeming factor of this career choice is it put me under the wing of my first radiology mentor.

Dr. David Witten was chairman of the radiology department at the time, a preeminent uroradiologist and a kind and gentle man. His practical approach was summed up in my favorite quote, "A normal calyx should be so sharp you can pick your teeth with it."

After about eighteen months of radiology training under Dr. Witten, the Navy decided I had had enough. They sent me to be the general medical officer on the USS *Nashville*, a ship with occasionally sick personnel and no radiology equipment. Do not do a radiology internship if there is any chance you will be a ship's doctor. A long course in sexually transmitted diseases would be much more useful.

Ultimately, I enjoyed general practice and stayed with it for about five years before returning to radiology as a resident at Bethesda Naval Hospital. There I worked with two more uroradiologists whom I would consider mentors, Dr. E. S. Amis and Dr. David Hartman. Both men are terrific radiologists, but each taught me very different things.

Dr. Amis was chairman of our department. He did not try to make life easy for us, which was not particularly appreciated at the time. Getting things done right, making a contribution to patient care and knowing what you need to know were far more important than feeling good. "Lunch is not a God-given right" was pretty characteristic. Still, I can not use a "radiologic hedge" phrase in my reports without worrying what Dr. Amis will think if he ever reads it, which, in the current legal climate, means I think of Steve Amis almost every day.

Dr. Hartman was the Navy radiologist at the Armed Forces Institute of Pathology. As residents at Bethesda, we knew him both in our department and at the AFIP. His calm and logical approach to a differential problem is something I am still trying to master. But more importantly, when you talked to him you knew he was listening, even though he had probably heard your unique and thoughtful question from other residents 7,000 times.

This year at the RSNA meeting, infoRad was filled with powerful new computer-based teaching systems that are obviously going to alter medical and radiologic training. New textbooks are coming out at an unbelievable rate. But the real art of radiology—things like approaching a clinical problem, finishing an exam on a patient in pain, making your department function as a team and dealing with know-it-all referring physicians—will always be taught by mentors.

How Do You Stack Up Against the Literature?

Maybe it's my imagination, but it seems that every month there is a new journal being introduced to the radiology community. This is good, because there are still a few areas in my office that are not yet stacked with unread radiology literature.

When I first got out of my residency I was gung-ho about keeping up. I bought books like mad. I read, shredded and filed articles from all the major journals. It took about three months to figure out that I would never again be as current or erudite as I was in the posh Executive West Hotel.

In spite of the surge in new publications, I find myself increasingly selective in what I even bother to unwrap. Most of my mail doesn't get opened, but I'm still a sucker for those contests where you have to find and lick seventy-five stamps so you can win $10 million. There are also a few journals I at least attempt to get through on a regular basis.

Radiographics is particularly good since it is highly visual. Some of the articles get a little wordy, but I usually just skim those parts. If you do any MRI at all you get used to the idea of looking at three hundred pictures for every line of clinical information generated.

The yellow and gray journals fit my classic idea of a radiology journal. I have received both intermittently over the years, and I find that I am much better at reading the abstracts than the actual articles. Unfortunately, most of the articles are out on the cutting edge of radiology, and I am back on the handle.

Perhaps it is a sign of some inner dissatisfaction, but I usually read the classified ads at the back of the gray journal, even though I have no intention of changing jobs. I'm looking for one that says, "Waterfront practice. 9 a.m. to 1 p.m. No nights, weekends or holidays. 250K." At that point I would be faced with a tough decision.

Most subspecialties have their own journal, often published by the subspecialty's organization. I find these remarkably useless in my practice except for the one dealing with my favorite area, ultrasound. Even here it seems most of the articles are of most importance to the people who can list them on their CVs.

I seem to be getting a lot more ads for "journals" published by book publishers and university presses, edited by noted academics and offering CME credits. For a big chunk of change, I can get four to six "highly focused, up-to-date, very practical" issues with X number of CME hours available. I'm sure there is a lot of useful information in these publications and the CME credits are earned, but I still feel like I'm buying a Rolex from a street vendor.

The number of what I have always called throwaway journals is on the rise as well. My partners tell me I have given a whole new meaning to that term since I started writing this column. My own definition of throwaway is a magazine that I actually read and then toss, occasionally saving an article or two. This is in contrast with the larger, dryer academic volumes, which often just get stacked on my desk until they can be added to the reference shelf.

Journals that do not use the "peer review" process are also sometimes lumped in the throwaway group. Peer review is highly touted by many in academic medicine. Of course, on college campuses there is nearly universal praise for sororities and fraternities—among the Greeks.

Even among academicians there is not universal praise for peer review. Readability can suffer with multiple reviewers. There is actually an index of readability, the Gunning-Fog index. A typical peer-reviewed medical journal might rate a 16, versus the editorial page of the *New York Times* at 11 and a standard legal contract at 18. Personally, I prefer as little fog as possible.

There is clearly no shortage of informative reading from which to choose. What I find in short supply is the time to read. I keep several piles of journals on my desk to deceive myself into believing I am keeping up with the literature. Of course, when half of them are still in their plastic wrap, the deception is a little less convincing.

ER Doc Eager To Set the Record Straight

Every Thursday, local emergency room physician Dr. Joe Murphy answers your medical questions. If you have a question send it to Dr. Joe, c/o the *Daily News*, Teetersville, SC 34410.

Dear Dr. Joe,

I am a big fan of the TV show "ER." I never realized how versatile you ER physicians are. How can you stay so cool? Sign me Impressed.

Dear Impressed,

I'm a big fan of the show too! It reminds me how exciting and important my work is! After college and medical school, ER doctors like myself undergo four long years of additional intensive training! So it isn't surprising that we can do virtually every medical procedure on earth by ourselves! Even the federal government has realized this and will now pay us for procedures that used to require specialists!

Dear Dr. Joe,

Last Tuesday we took our son to the ER for a bad cough that had been bothering him for a week. We were there almost five hours. What gives? Sign me Upset.

Dear Upset,

You should be upset! Unfortunately, I don't control the entire hospital yet, but rest assured that my nurses and I are looking at every department supporting us to see who to blame for your delay!

Dear Dr. Joe,

The last time I was in the Emergency Room I noticed that everyone, including the lady cleaning the floor, had a stethoscope draped around their neck. Is there a reason? Sign me Confused.

Dear Confused,

As a midget football coach I like to say, "It takes a team to play a team sport!" In the ER we are a team—we look the look and we speak the speak! Besides, it doesn't take a cardiologist to listen to a heart! I can teach anyone how to do it in thirty minutes!

Dear Dr. Joe,

When my mom came in for her chest cold she had a chest X-ray done in her ER room bed. Later, when she was admitted to the hospital, she had to go down to radiology for her chest X-rays. Why not do them all in bed? Sign me Inconvenienced.

Dear Inconvenienced,

I'm sorry to hear your mom had to get out of her hospital bed! You and I know that a chest X-ray is a chest X-ray! However, some hospital personnel are not quite the "team players" we would like them to be! I don't want to point fingers, but if certain radiology technologists and doctors would realize that speed and convenience are top priorities, nice people like your mom could get all their X-rays done in bed!

Dear Dr. Joe,

Last week my cousin Tommy Ray and I walked over from Boonsville to get his neck pain checked out. As soon as he got checked into the ER your staff wrapped a collar around his neck, strapped him on a board and rushed him over to get X-rays. He got front-of-the-line privileges! I know if he had gone to see our family doctor he would have needed an appointment. Sign me Happy in Boonsville.

Dear Happy,

It's always nice to hear from a satisfied patient! Patients seen by their family doctor may think they're sick, but when you come to the ER we know you are more important! Rest assured that we will always insist that our patients come first, and we won't stop until every last diagnostic possibility has been tested!

Dear Dr. Joe,

Recently I brought my mom in after she fell on the ice. You checked her over, X-rayed her hip, gave us a prescription, and sent her home to rest for a week. The next day we were called back because some radiologist thought she needed more tests on her hip. We ended up spending a lot of money on tests and surgery that you wanted to avoid in the first place. Sign me Ticked in Teetersville.

Dear Ticked,

I'm sorry to hear you had so much trouble with your mom's injury! That kind of thing used to happen occasionally. Hopefully, now that we can take care of your mom's problem completely in the ER, that kind of hassle can be avoided! With the support of the federal government, it shouldn't be long before the only specialist you'll ever need is your local ER physician!

Too Much Style, Or Not Enough?

One of my routine tasks I enjoy least is proofreading my reports. Several times a day I am presented with piles of verbiage that I have generated. Unfortunately, I am a very poor proofreader. I tend to go very fast and often seem to correct mistakes in my mind without ever really seeing them. There is also the temptation to just read the "impression," since I know that this is the only part most of my referring physicians read.

When I do go slowly—or worse yet, when I have to read a report I dictated years ago—I am often amazed at what I have said. In an effort to be helpful, insightful, reasonable, fast, thorough, and not liable, I frequently say some pretty stupid things.

There are the obvious mistakes, like broken fibulas in the wrist and meibomian cysts on the cervix. These slips of the tongue are usually funny, but they do make you look sort of dumb if they make it to the patient's chart. What I find more embarrassing are many of the styles and techniques I (and a lot of radiologists) use to communicate both what I know and what I don't.

There is an easy way to describe a finding. There is more than one way, in fact. There is, however, one way we all use too much. There is a need for variety in your sentence structure. There is a real tendency for the reader to ignore what you are saying if you begin every sentence the same way.

In the Navy I worked with a radiologist who liked to give long, flowing descriptions of every detail on the film. Unfortunately, he seldom added an interpretation or conclusion to these descriptions. This had two major drawbacks: His reports were overly long, and they were useless. I occasionally find myself slipping into this pattern, particularly if I am completely stumped as to what is actually going on with the case. Adding "the etiology is not apparent" somewhere in your impression seems more honest.

Some people dictate from the hip. They describe findings and interpret those findings as they skip through the body of their report. When they get to the end they add "Impression, see above." I hate this. It is like reading badly written assembly instructions for a toy—go to part A1, go to part A2, now go back to part A1. Instead, I try to read the images, make up my mind, and then give a conclusion.

Early in my career, I was fond of radiologic jargon. General practitioners don't really care about the "silhouette sign" or "Golden's S sign." They do care if there is a lingular infiltrate or a hilar mass, and they really care if they have to waste time figuring out what you are trying to say. Now, I try to leave talking in obscure jargon to the real pros—lawyers.

I used to end some reports with "clinical correlation advised." What clinician with more than two firing neurons doesn't correlate every test with the clinical setting? Obviously, lab data, history, and physical exam can differentiate between two or more possibilities for a given radiographic abnormality. I try to say it a little differently because this particular phrase seems so obvious it is almost insulting. It reminds me of the statement "Caution, coffee is hot" that companies like McDonald's put on their cups after some clumsy person sues them.

Read one of your screening mammo reports. Is it a nice succinct report followed by a half-page disclaimer? Does your disclaimer basically say "Breast cancers can be hard to see, we're doing the best we can, please don't sue us."? We all know that no one is perfect, but thanks to our amazing legal system, we are compelled to whine about it on our reports. If these disclaimers had any legal value they would be understandable, but I am told that they don't, so they just seem like a banner expressing a lack of self-confidence.

I have to remind myself constantly, whether I am writing fiction, non-fiction, or radiology reports (which may contain elements of both): What I write reflects on me and the quality of my work. And what I write also says, indirectly, what I think of my reader.

Good CME Should Do More Than Brain Tweak

I am a great believer in CME courses, for a variety of reasons. We all know that radiology is changing at a breathtaking pace. While I am inundated with books and journals containing what I need to know, I find myself distracted by more urgent, but less important, tasks on a daily basis. At a CME course, it is easier to concentrate on improving my skills, and there is usually something more fun than "call" to do in the evening.

Apparently, there are rewards for the people who put on these courses. How else can you explain the exponential growth in the number of courses and the tuition charges? All this competition for your CME dollars means that the standard of care is pretty high. Unfortunately, like most medical products, competition has not lowered the price, but it does provide for variety and overall high quality.

I make it to at least two courses a year, and often go to three or four. Over the years my criteria for choosing which courses to attend have changed. Dates, sponsoring institution, specific lecturers, location, cost, and number of CME credits are all things I consider.

Being in an eight-person group has made scheduling anything in my life much more difficult. In a three-person group I could usually whine my way out of a week at the last minute. Now, unless I plan way in advance (which I have always considered a sin), there is a high probability that I won't be able to get the particular week off that I want. Fortunately, there are companies that offer the same pseudo-course every week in twenty different places for last-minute planners like me.

Who is sponsoring the meeting makes a difference. When the Armed Forces Institute of Pathology (AFIP) puts on a meeting, you know that you'll get lots of radiologic-pathologic correlation. You also know that there will be lots of gorgeous slides in finely honed and practiced lectures. If you go to a Harvard course in Boston, take your smart pills. You are going to be inundated with information all day long. Harvard courses away from Boston seem a little less obsessive-compulsive.

Specific speakers often attract me to a course. There are people I have heard many times, and I like their style. I know I will learn something from them, assuming they are not repeating the same lecture. Actually, even hearing the same lecture again can be useful, depending upon where my mind was the first time I "heard" it. There seem to be a growing number of professional lecturers. I see their names in so many brochures, I wonder how they have time to practice radiology.

Everyone has different criteria for what constitutes a good lecture. For me, a lecturer should entertain, not just cover a topic. There are a number of ways to make a lecture interesting, but I prefer humor. I don't expect a Bill Cosby routine, but the mental break created by a chuckle every five minutes or so has a profound influence on the attention level of most audiences. Enthusiasm for the topic—both the lecturer's and the audience's—also seems to make a lecture more entertaining. There are some people who are just so crazy and/or flamboyant you have to listen to them. But it never fails: Every course has at least one speaker about as exciting as a "B" reading.

The number of CME hours offered is increasingly important for me. I don't like too many hours. Perhaps it is age, or maybe my fondness for merlots, but I reach a point of diminishing returns after four or five hours of lectures in a day. I still go to courses featuring eight hours of lectures a day, but I am selective about the ones I attend. This is especially true after lunch, when my postprandial cerebral oxygen deficiency kicks in.

More and more I find myself thinking like a real estate agent—location, location, location. There are so many courses on any given subject, I now spend as much time deciding where I want to go as what I want to hear. Put me near a nice beach or in a fun city, and give me four hours of interesting and entertaining lectures each morning. Then my brain will be tweaked, my body will be happy, and the IRS will leave me alone.

When Proactive Becomes Overreactive

Every article or book I read dealing with change, whether it be healthcare reform, managed care, or mid-life, tells me that I need to take the initiative, not be reactive. But how do you get proactive when everyone around you is lighting a fire? You have to react or get torched.

The current pyromaniacs in my hospital are the surgeons. About six months ago we purchased a digital stereotactic breast biopsy machine. Before we bought it, we worked out an algorithm under which any patient with a positive mammogram would first consult a surgeon, and then have a stereotactic breast biopsy (SBB) or a needle localization, as the surgeon saw fit. As our group's experience grows, the number of needle locs has diminished for some surgeons as the number of stereotactic biopsies has gone up.

Last week one of the surgeons attended a seven-hour course and applied for privileges to do stereotactic biopsies. It never occurred to us that someone who has never been trained to read mammograms would feel qualified to do a mammographic procedure. But then, he did have seven hours of training. Maybe those hours are like accelerated dog years—seven hours of surgical training equals 490 hours of radiology training.

Looking back, I believe we made several mistakes in establishing our biopsy program. Our primary error was placing hospital politics above patient care. From the patient's perspective, a well-done stereotactic biopsy is always preferable to an open biopsy. To appease surgeons threatened by SBB, we placed unnecessary hurdles for our patients between a positive mammogram and a definitive diagnosis by SBB. A woman with a positive mammogram wants and deserves a quick definitive answer, not an obstacle course.

We were also naive. My partners and I would never consider trying to do laparoscopic surgery after a one-day course. How can one expect to do accurate mammographic biopsies without knowing how to read mammograms? I know the American College of Surgeons is interested in continuity of care, providing full service to their patients and other glowing purposes, but they sound like life insurance salespeople who tell me they are only interested in my security. Everyone likes the color green, no matter what they say.

Our "exclusive" contract with the hospital gave us a false sense of security. When we pointed out to the administration that credentialing someone outside our group would violate our contract, their response was enlightening. They said that our contract excluded other radiologists, but not other specialties—a very creative interpretation. They also implied that we might win this battle, but lose the war if our contract didn't get renewed. Now that is a legal document you can really depend on.

If you are planning to start an SBB program at your hospital, I would offer the following advice. First, send some of your radiologists to Steve Parker and Fred Burbank's modestly entitled course on SBB, "Breast Imaging and Intervention Into the 21st Century." The first time you hear Steve speak, you will understand where the program name originated. The course raises and answers all the important questions about starting your biopsy program. I went six months after our program started, which is pretty typical of my timing throughout life.

When you establish your program, make training in mammography a credentialing criterion. The hard part of this procedure is not firing the biopsy gun; the cleaning staff can do that. Real problems arise in determining whether to proceed with biopsy and finding the lesion on the digital image: mammographic problems. Make everyone who wants to do SBB prove that they have these skills. The only official criteria I know are those promulgated by the MQSA—not my favorite piece of legislation, but why not use them?

Most importantly, think of your patients first. Use the opportunity to redesign your mammography program with the best interests of patients as your top priority. Try to eliminate every sleepless night a woman has between a questionable mammogram and a definitive answer. Then, when your surgeons light this fire—and you know they will—at least you'll be fighting it from the high ground.

Left and Right: There Is a Difference

It seems like a simple thing, but the issue of right versus left causes quite a few headaches in my department. Patients, doctors, and technologists alike—no one can consistently tell one hand from the other.

All day long when I am doing fluoro, I have to correct my patients. "Please turn a little to your left. No, your other left, please." I must constantly remind myself these people are not stupid, just anxious.

Our technologists are always being reminded to use their metal film markers. Unfortunately, we now have right and left stickers to be used on those rare occasions when repeating an unlabeled film is not possible. It is interesting how some techs have several "impossible to repeat" situations every day, while others never have any.

Of course, using the metal film markers doesn't guarantee perfect results. I think mislabeled films are the real reason someone invented those little date stickers. Whenever I see two or three date stickers on a film, I know someone is covering his or her tracks. All the date stickers in the world won't disguise the sound of a metal marker fed into the daylight processor.

Since moving into our new hospital, a new right/left problem has arisen. Our department has several automated film viewers. In the past we all read from a stack, but now most of our films are hung on multiviewers by the technologists as they are done. This is extremely convenient and efficient. But all radiologists have their own preferences about the correct way to hang films. In my department, I seem to be the only one who knows the right way.

In truth, I am not very picky about how things are hung; I just appreciate the fact that I spend far less time handling films. But many radiologists are more particular. Some radiologists want all lateral views pointing to the left, some want them all to the right. Others want all films in anatomic position with the lateral views facing the direction of the marker. I wonder if this obsession with one side or the other is the result of their residency training or their toilet training.

Mammogram reports are another place where right and left errors often show up. I can't count the number of times I have given what I felt was a brilliant and erudite description and evaluation of a subtle breast abnormality, and then concluded by recommending further evaluation of the wrong breast. Fortunately, most of our transcriptionists know one hand from the other. And if they don't catch it, my error is painfully obvious to the referring physician.

The emergency room is often a source of wrong-side errors. Our X-ray requests are transmitted from the ER to us via computer. When the patient arrives, our techs have a printed request in hand, and they know they are supposed to do exactly what is requested.

"Hi, Mr. Smith, I'm going to be doing some X-rays of your right forearm."

"Why?" asks Mr. Smith, looking incredulously at his left arm, which takes a 90 degree turn at mid-radius level.

Perhaps because of recent publicized cases, patients are often very attentive to which side is being examined. My techs are frequently questioned by patients who want to know why they have their left side against the X-ray film when it is their right chest that hurts. People forget that X-rays go right through them.

Labeling sides correctly is very important in ultrasound as well. It is so operator-dependent that just about anything can be created or eliminated at the whim of the person holding the transducer. If you don't scan your patients at least briefly yourself, you should avoid aggravating your sonographer, who can make you look really stupid before you ever know what hit you.

Right and left errors are common in all walks of life. Who hasn't been given directions and later found out the person meant to say "right turn"? But like so much of radiology, our right/left mistakes seem glaringly obvious because we capture them on film.

SBFT? I'd Rather Be Diagnosing Elsewhere

Small bowel follow-through exams are not my favorite study. Once the barium passes the C-loop, I'm in no-man's-land until it reaches the ileocecal valve.

I did an informal survey of my partners to see how many SBFT exams we had done over our cumulative careers and how many Meckel's diverticula we had diagnosed. We estimated a total of 10,000 exams. Using the "rule of twos," we should have seen one hundred Meckel's. The rule says that two percent of the population have a Meckel's within two feet of the ileocecal valve, and that whenever you ask radiologists how many of a procedure they have done they will multiply the number by two. That we have seen less than five Meckel's didn't surprise me. What I read and hear about small bowel disease doesn't always apply to my practice.

My favorite GI book is Eisenberg's—great pictures, nice lists, and a very methodical approach to the GI tract. He beautifully discusses dozens of small bowel disorders. But having reread these chapters many times, I still find that the only small bowel diagnoses I make are Crohn's, lymphoma, and obstruction.

I have heard several excellent lectures on "Approaches to Small Bowel Disease," "Small Bowel Diseases Made Easy," and others. When I hear such lectures, I have a clear understanding of how to separate these diseases—at least until I do my next SBFT.

This seems to be a popular lecture topic for alumni of the Armed Forces Institute of Pathology. I suspect that's because they are some of the few people who can accumulate enough interesting examples of the pathology. I often wonder how many of the cases were diagnosed preoperatively on the basis of the small bowel films. Even I can characterize the small bowel pattern when I know the diagnosis.

A lot of radiology boils down to knowing normal from abnormal. The most frequently consulted book in radiology is probably Keats' *Atlas of Normal Roentgen Variants That May Simulate Disease*, 9,000th edition.

I think that is why I feel so defeated by the small intestine. Everything looks a little disease-simulating.

If it isn't Crohn's or obstruction I often end up asking my partners, "Does this look funny to you?" Unfortunately, they usually say something like "Yeah. Well, maybe. But I don't think it's Crohn's. Is there a history of lymphoma?"

Small bowel transit time is a problem for many reasons. I was trained to get films every fifteen or twenty minutes and fluoro several times during the exam. But trying to fit that into a busy fluoro schedule can be maddening, especially if you have four SBFT exams in one morning. Inevitably, someone doesn't get the film on time and all of a sudden I'm looking at a useless antegrade study of the colon. The only predictor of transit time I know is when the study is started; exams added on late in the day inevitably have the motility of a dead snake.

Flocculation is a sign that everyone talks about, but they always say, "This used to be a reliable sign, but not anymore. The new bariums have eliminated this finding." I've been hearing this since 1978. Apparently, back in the days of flocculation, small bowel diseases were so easily distinguished my granny could do it.

Our technologists are equally fond of small bowel studies. Very few referring physicians tell their patients what to expect, and how long to allocate, when coming for an SBFT. Patients are often "excited" to learn that they may be in our department for two or three hours, and guess who gets blamed?

Some of our referring physicians must think we are magicians. They send us semicomatose patients on hyperalimentation who haven't had oral intake in this century, and we're supposed to give them four cups of barium without a nasogastric tube?

Fortunately, the SBFT is being replaced by the much more accurate small bowel enema or enteroclysis. This allows us to spend five times as long performing studies that are almost always negative. I have come to the conclusion that enteroclysis is one of those studies best performed by experts, so now if someone asks about an SBFT before ordering the exam, I can happily refer the patient for a better test.

Retirement Planning Made Not-So-Easy

Managed care is bringing a wide range of changes to the practice of medicine and doctor's careers. Dealing with these changes has forced radiologists to examine how they do studies, why they do studies, and when they should or should not do studies. But it seems that now more than ever, they are thinking about when they can stop doing studies. Everyone is talking about retirement and retirement funds.

There is a proliferation of articles about planning for financial security. These articles are filled with both general advice and specific formulas for calculating what I need to set aside for my retirement. To stop working, live comfortably, and deal with inflation, I figure I need about $1 billion in my 401(k). So I set up a professionally-managed account. Based on its performance to date, I'll only need to contribute $2 billion to reach my goal.

The partners in my group have "self-directed" retirement funds. That means I get to choose which drain I want my money to go down. When I first started contributing to my plan, I entrusted my money to a local stockbroker. It took about three years to realize that his investment strategy was selling me whatever the main office was pushing. I then changed to another professional, who was able to keep me breaking even during two years when the Dow Jones average made amazing gains.

Bad performance in the stock market is nothing new to me. In 1987, all my friends were making money in stocks, so in October I bought my first stocks. The following Monday, Oct. 19, was Black Monday. The largest drop since the Depression cut my investment in half. Obviously an omen, but I ignored it.

During my ten years in the Navy, I didn't worry about my retirement fund. Once a year, I would get a memo from the Pentagon. It told me how much all the perks I got as a military doctor were worth, so I wouldn't feel bad that my salary was one-third that of my civilian counterparts. The amount I was saving on country club dues, civilian work clothes, exotic travel, etc., really boosted my income. The biggest plus was my retirement fund. Unfortunately, if you leave before twenty years of service, that big plus becomes a big goose egg.

I gave a lot of thought to the retirement fund question before leaving the Navy. It seemed to me that twenty years of contributions at a private practice income level would offset my lost years in the Navy. I didn't realize that everyone in the country would be trying to make my income go down, or make a commission every time I even looked at my retirement account.

Even though I don't like being involved with the stock market, it seems to be the primary place for retirement investments these days. Chinchilla farming has passed its peak, and I don't have enough room to raise llamas or ostriches.

The stock market is like those sirens on the rocks: It keeps luring me back. "Come on over here. You can make a lot of money. Sure, there is a little risk, but don't worry, we have some professional advisors here to help you." Professional advisors have lost me a lot of money. But like traditional medicine, it doesn't matter how I do, they still get paid. What about a system where the advisor's income is based on my success? That sounds a lot like one of the arguments for managed care, but it is callous to compare healthcare and investment counseling, so I think medicine should stick to fee-for-service.

Two years ago I got a little relief from an unexpected source. Our group hired a new interventional radiologist. I used to do some basic interventional stuff, but having no desire to do angioplasties, TIPS, etc., I was quite willing to relinquish these procedures. He seems to know his subspecialty, but more importantly, he really knows the stock market. Since I started relying on his advice, my account has done much better.

This has some important ramifications. The job market in radiology is getting tight. If I were a senior resident, I would strongly consider a fellowship in investing, or better still, get an MBA. A lot of groups would jump at someone advertising himself as a radiologist/portfolio manager.

Sports and Medicine: Too Close For Comfort

It was hard not to get caught up in the excitement of the Olympics. Everywhere I turned I was hit with another ad for the official airline, the official snack, or the official toilet bowl cleaner of the Olympics. Remembering the Summer Games of my youth, I couldn't help thinking about the changes in both sports and medicine. We're a little behind the athletes, but we are definitely entering the commercial era.

I don't remember a single athlete competing in sunglasses twenty years ago, but then no one sold sunglasses in those days for $200.

Logos were everywhere at the '96 Olympics. TV reporters interpreted every medal won or lost in terms of a windfall or disaster in future advertising revenue. The competitors may be dedicated to their sports, but there is increasing emphasis on the commercial value of every achievement. I can't be critical of them, since they, like us in medicine, are just dealing with the realities of changing times.

Not long ago physicians established a reputation for excellence through consistent good work. Be it research, teaching, or clinical acumen, you relied on the opinion of others and word-of-mouth to determine your value to the medical community. In the new competitive marketplace, physicians, and more conspicuously healthcare organizations, are feeling a need for self-promotion that rivals the NBA's.

Physicians and groups seem more inclined to place ads in the phone book and local newspaper, or send out self-aggrandizing press releases about topics in their specialties. HMOs are more subtle—like a giant apple core lesion. Millions of "healthcare dollars" are being spent on major ad campaigns featuring warm and fuzzy images of pregnant women, newborn babies, and old people spending their retirement in Shangri-la. I probably wouldn't mind so much if I didn't believe that those millions are coming out of the pockets of the people who are actually providing the care.

Unless Congress takes action, which is like hoping for a pelvic ultrasound patient's bladder to fill without a foley at 2:00 A.M., we will probably see the consolidation of America's healthcare into a relatively small number of very profitable corporations. When this happens, you can be sure the marketing departments will be far better funded than radiology or surgery. I suspect that in some HMOs they already are.

Naturally, the marketers will want to glamorize some positions. Traditionally, fields like neurosurgery and cardiac surgery have attracted the big publicity, the big bucks, and the big egos. But the major payors are now pushing primary-care physicians as the medical quarterbacks, pitchers, and singles champions, so the marketing departments are bound to follow.

Planted articles about how Dr. Friendly overcame chronic rhinorrhea to become a famous internist, and Oprah shows devoted to the mental stress of family practice will become commonplace.

Consolidation into giant teams may be a few years off, but large insurance companies already act like major league coaches and managers. They want to call the plays from the sidelines while sending others out to do the work and take the hits. If the actions they direct end in disaster, they blame the players. The best part is they control the purse strings, so they can pay themselves first.

Perhaps the trend will continue to the point that physicians become valuable property for the healthcare giants. They would love to have the right to "retire" us at their leisure. Physicians will get traded from team to team, unless you're good enough to negotiate as a free agent. Then the real money starts to flow—endorsing consumer products, making personal appearances, and wearing trendy logos on your uniform while you work. Some companies might pay us to wear their competitors' logos while we do barium enemas.

My aspirations go beyond subspecialty certification, being a free agent, and wearing logos on my uniform. Like most baby boomers, I'm trying to diet and exercise myself out of the reality of growing older. So I'm hoping eventually to have a series of magazine ads featuring me in Oakley sunglasses, designer underwear, and my flashy lead apron.

And Now, Our Program Host, Dr. Brad!

For the past few years, the American College of Radiology has offered a special training session at its annual meeting on dealing with the media. Interest in this sort of thing is growing as we enter medicine's corporate era. I haven't attended the course yet, but I have added it to my list of things I need to do. It may be a few years, though, since what I need to do and what I actually do seldom overlap. Besides, I've been teaching myself, and we know the ACR is big on home study.

How am I preparing to ride this new wave of medicine into the twenty-first century? I'm watching lots of infomercials. I'm also whitening my teeth and honing my motivational speaking skills so I can be a TV authority.

You're saying, "Brad, medical infomercials are for ginseng products and hair follicle stimulators. Legitimate medical practitioners don't advertise like that." I agree. I'm not talking about legitimate providers; I'm talking about giant HMOs and healthcare corporations.

Can't you imagine a group of attractive and vivacious doctors, nurses, and professional models being interviewed in front of a paid audience about the joys of being an employee or patient at Blue Square/Blue Circle Medicine?

"They were so concerned about me when I went in for my X-rays," says the young lady into the camera. "When I complained about the taste of the barium, the technologist drank it for me."

As the show's host, I get to ask spontaneous probing and intellectual questions, with equally spontaneous probing and intellectual rehearsed answers. "Dr. Shrewdblade, are you and your staff keeping up with the latest surgical advances?"

"Glad you asked that, Brad. Just yesterday my staff and I were discussing even more uses for our wonderful laser. I brought one of my patients with me today who can tell you how we remodeled her body, removed all her nonessential organs, and cleaned her teeth—without ever using a knife."

These "laser" interviews are very important in modern medicine. It seems that most patients believe anything done with a laser will turn out perfectly, and not hurt. I think some marketing people have done a good job. I can't remember the last time I saw an ad for a procedure done with "a really sharp knife."

The studio audience segments will be broken up by video vignettes patterned after the "up close and personal" interviews done ad nauseam at the Olympics. I can walk around the hospital interviewing good-looking doctors and nurses, asking inane questions about the facility.

"This MRI scanner is really impressive-looking. Tell us, Mr. Technologist, what does it do?"

"Well, with patients located in a strong magnetic field, we expose them to various combinations of radio waves and changing magnetic fields in order to generate a signal from their shifting protons, which we convert into spatially localized data points," says Mr. Technologist.

"Could you put that into layman's terms?"

"We microwave them in a magnet."

Administrators know that patients form a special bond with a hospital if their children are born there. So naturally I'll do lots of interviews in the delivery area. It is easy to do TV shows there, because the modern birthing suite is palatial. The only larger and nicer rooms in the hospital are in the administrative wing. This is in contrast to radiology, where the rooms are actually designed to shrink a few inches every year.

Large healthcare entities may even create their own phone-in cable channels, like the home shopping networks.

"Hi, this is Dr. Brad on the Geyser Infermemente Network. How can we help you?"

"Hi, Dr. Brad. This is Joe from Billings, Montana. I've been having chest pain."

"Thanks for calling, Joe. Does it hurt on your left side?"

"Yes it does, Dr. Brad."

"Joe, I've set you up for a thallium scan at your local Geyser clinic and I'm phoning in a prescription for nitro tablets. Let's go to our next caller, a swollen leg from North Carolina."

A final media format that has intrigued me for years is used on the PBS radio show "Car Talk." Two intelligent and very funny brothers answer listeners' questions about problems with their cars. I really like this show, but I'm afraid it may not be the route for me. First, I would actually have to know a lot of medicine, and second, the days of doing anything for free in healthcare are probably over.

Shedding Light on Viewbox Reading

Our department administrator recently sent out a memo on the future integration of PACS in our department. It was a well-thought-out explanation for the phased introduction of PACS into our workplace. I didn't like it. I like viewboxes.

Viewboxes are an important part of radiology. They have evolved over time into sophisticated and functional devices. They are not perfect, but I don't want to give them up. I do my best work at a viewbox, and I do some pretty fair radiology there, too.

I like to let my mind wander in front of a viewbox. Not just any viewbox; it has to be filled with films. Otherwise, there is too much ambient light. You can't daydream in front of an eight-panel box with a few extremity films in the middle. You need it filled with 14 x 17 chest or abdomen films. Then the light level is low enough that you can drift off on a creative or problem-solving tangent and not fry your retinas.

Some might think letting your mind wander at the viewbox is dangerous, like a trucker falling asleep on the interstate. I believe these mental breaks are productive, as long as you disengage your mouth when you disengage your brain—like the trucker who pulls into a rest area to nap.

The best part is that you look like you're working. I have taken this technique one step further: I can wander off mentally for ages holding a magnifying glass between my face and the film. People hesitate to interrupt you if you're "working" that studiously. And if they do interrupt, you can get irritated. How many jobs are there where you can act indignant if someone disturbs your daydreaming?

There are some modifications I would make to viewboxes. My portable computer has an automatic dimming device. If I don't use it for several minutes, it automatically dims the screen to conserve energy. I'm not sure that dimming a viewbox would save much energy, because they use fluorescent bulbs, and I've never really understood how they work. (Voodoo, I think.) But I know my eyeballs would appreciate one, and it would be nice for other radiologists in rooms with more than one reading station.

A small recess to hold your coffee cup would be nice. The new lecture hall at the Armed Forces Institute of Pathology in Washington, DC, has a large cup holder built into the desk at each chair. This is a great idea. What radiologist hasn't had a cup of coffee (occasionally hot) spilled on his or her desk/films/reports/lap? Your films get sticky. Your transcriptionists think you're a fool when you ask them to redo a batch of reports with no typos. You have to walk around with a brown stain for the rest of the day. And no matter how much you wipe it up, the next time you lay a film down, you find a puddle you missed.

Viewboxes need to be designed to hold films hanging only from the top edge. Strings and grooves at the bottom are okay as supplemental restraints, but when someone brings you a film for a quick look, you want to pop it up under a clip on the top. A lot of motorized viewers require that the bottom edge and sometimes the strings be used, even for a brief hanging. We have one viewer that is particularly frustrating in this regard. If you stick a film in the top edge it feels secure, but when you let go, the film drops into the bowels of the machine. We've had this machine almost two years, but I still feed it films at least once a week.

The bulbs in a viewbox need to be wired in series, like old Christmas tree lights. When one bulb goes out, the whole viewer is useless. That would get the attention of whoever is supposed to change the bulbs. As it is now, if one light goes out, it is a low-priority problem on everyone else's list. The radiologist who is driven bonkers by it sounds like one of the Whiners from "Saturday Night Live" if he mentions it more than once during the day.

I know it is inevitable that film will ultimately be replaced by an electronic medium for image archiving, etc. Otherwise, why would all the big film companies be spending fortunes on R&D in this area? But the rate of change in my practice and my life in general has gotten so fast, I am starting to identify with my elderly patients who resist any change, just because it is a change. And I'm also worried. I was raised in the TV era. I was parked in front of a TV for much of my childhood. An atom bomb can't draw my attention away from an active cathode ray tube. How will I continue writing (and subconsciously solve a lot of my problems) if I can't daydream in front of a PACS screen?

1997

You Decide: Frozen North or Radiological Fun in the Sun?

Every year I go to the RSNA meeting in Chicago. I like the refresher courses, infoRad, the scientific exhibits, some of the papers, and most of all, the atmosphere of the event. It makes you realize how large and diverse our field is, but you see enough old friends and colleagues to remind you we really are a community. Diagnostic Imaging covers the meeting extensively, so I use that as another excuse to go.

It was in this spirit of professional education and journalistic inquiry that I attended the October InterAmerican Congress of Radiology, jointly sponsored by the RSNA, the Colegio Interamericano de Radiologia and the Federacion Mexicana de Radiologia e Imagen. This was the first year the RSNA had participated in the meeting, and I was curious how the two meetings would compare. Having to spend a week in Cancun, Mexico, did not detract from the mission.

Since it was primarily a Latin American meeting, I encountered a few problems. When I received my registration material, it was all printed in Spanish. The neurons holding my one year of high school Spanish have apparently succumbed in a war with Chardonnay, but a Spanish-speaking friend helped me fill out the forms. Most of the lectures were in Spanish, but there was simultaneous translation into English (or vice versa for the English lectures). The Spanish-speaking lecturers seemed unaffected by this, while most of the North Americans felt they had to speak slowly and distinctly, like a third-grade teacher. I kept wishing they would talk faster, so I would have more to think about when I left to go snorkeling.

The influence of the RSNA on the meeting was obvious: The signage was impressive. If you've ever been to the Chicago meeting, you know what I'm talking about; they have signage on steroids. And there were lots of RSNA-style ribbons on the name tags in Cancun. I had one that said "Doesn't understand the monetary exchange system."

The scientific exhibits are one of the best parts of the RSNA meeting. You can, and I usually do, spend a day or two on them. About half the exhibits are excellent, while the rest should have the name of an airline on them, since they look like they were done primarily so the author would get a ticket to Chicago. The exhibits in Cancun were far less extensive, and they were in Spanish. I concentrated on the images, and then processed them on the beach.

Eating lunch at McCormick Place can be a challenge. There are always long lines of people waiting to buy fast food at outrageous prices. You get the quality of a mall food court, without the service or ambiance. At the InterAmerican Congress, after a two-minute walk I was lying on the beach, where all I had to do was say, "*Dos Coronas, por favor,*" and a friendly young man would bring me lunch.

The technical exhibits at the RSNA are overwhelming. Every piece of radiology equipment imaginable—and a lot of things you can't conceive of using on a human being—is on display. If you are in the market for major equipment, you really need to go to Chicago. But if you're looking for silver jewelry, T-shirts, hand-woven rugs, or anything printed with a tacky and/or vulgar slogan on it, Cancun is a better choice.

Unlike most trade shows, the RSNA does not allow exhibitors to give out freebies. I think this is one of those image things, like the size of the pepper grinder in trendy restaurants. Not so in Mexico. Long lines formed at the Kodak booth for free beach bags and beach balls. Personally, I can't see standing in line for thirty-five cents worth of junk. A couple of dollars maybe, but not thirty-five cents.

I read recently that the RSNA is considering a change of venue for the annual meeting. Apparently, they have a contract with Chicago through 2002, but are discussing a move to Orlando when it expires. The organization seems so entrenched in the Windy City that I have to wonder if this is a serious possibility, or just a way of haggling with the city over price. Personally, I like an excuse to go Christmas shopping in Chicago, and there are already so many medical meetings in Orlando that if you cough in a restaurant, half a dozen people try to Heimlich you.

No matter where they have it, I will still try to go to the RSNA meeting every year. It is just too important an event in radiology. But the InterAmerican Congress was an excellent experience, and it did a lot more for my tan lines.

Geek-Friendly PACS Not Always the Smartest Buy

In a recent column I mentioned that my department is taking a serious look at filmless radiology. With this in mind, one of my goals at last December's RSNA meeting (along with having fun, Christmas shopping, and eating some great meals) was to evaluate PACS. By my second day in Chicago, I realized I was only going to meet three of my four goals.

Several factors contributed to my inability to evaluate PACS. I thought I understood the basics from articles and lectures I've taken in over the last few years, and I was right. Unfortunately, this is the equivalent of memorizing a phrase book in a foreign language. I possessed enough knowledge to ask one semi-intelligent question, but I couldn't understand the answer. I asked a few suppliers, "Is your equipment DICOM-compatible?" This is like asking car salesmen if their cars run on gas.

A major problem is the sheer number of vendors building and selling PACS equipment and related paraphernalia. I think every brand name you have ever seen—GE, Siemens, Fuji, Chef Boyardee, Studebaker, etc.—has gotten into this field. And there are ten times as many unheard-of companies pushing their gear. The unheard-ofs are particularly hard to get a handle on, since their names are so much alike. Next year the new North Building opens at McCormick Place, with the floor space of ten baseball fields. It will probably be too small for all the PACS equipment.

I am a simple person. I never enjoyed building TVs from Heath kits or cars from spare parts. I like package deals, turnkey operations, and one-dish meals (if I'm cooking). A company that can sell me a complete system, already compatible with what we have, has a lot of appeal. There were about a million such systems on display in Chicago—but there were two million vendors selling individual components.

It reminds me of stereo equipment. I admit audiophiles can assemble individual components into a system of amazing quality and sound reproduction. I, on the other hand, have a system with the same brand name on every component. While the high-end system is probably better, I'm not sure I can appreciate the difference. But I know whom to call if something goes wrong with mine.

This problem of too many options does have its upside. There were a lot of people window-shopping at the RSNA meeting this year. Competition for the few radiology departments actually ready to spend real money should be keen, which may help keep prices reasonable. Best of all, buyers should demand one hundred percent money-back guarantees. If a company can't stand behind its product as well as the typical consumer mail-order catalog, perhaps it shouldn't be in the business. Such a satisfaction guarantee would also encourage salespeople to help determine the best system for your needs, not the most you can afford.

Since being overwhelmed by all this information, I have been wondering how to approach the PACS decision. The best way I came up with is not available to me, but if your group is lucky enough to include a computer geek, give that person the job of selecting the system. Be sure to try it before you buy it, though, since a system that is computer-geek-friendly is not necessarily user-friendly.

Another option is to hire an impartial consultant who knows the field. Let the consultant help you figure how to begin attacking this technologic behemoth. But don't overlook the step of trying out the system, because anyone good enough to be a consultant in this field has to harbor a little computer geekism.

A third option (this one has a certain appeal to me) is to use the old-school approach to radiology equipment purchases. Call up the two or three equipment sales reps you know really well, and ask them what they have that will get you into PACS. Let them wine and dine you at the RSNA meeting, and take you on some site visits. Then pick one from this limited sample. Since any system you buy today will probably be obsolete in a few years, why not enjoy the selection process?

This decision involves a lot of money, both invested in the equipment and potentially saved if we make the right choice. Such decisions are made well below the speed of light in my hospital, since any purchase over $500 has to be approved by every committee, administrator, and grandmother within one hundred miles. I'm counting on five or ten more trips to Chicago to study the field before a decision is made. By then most of the weak horses should be out of the race, and I might understand the equipment.

The More Things Change, the More They Change

Who came up with the term "interventional radiology"? Why not "really messy radiology"? Or "nothing-ever-goes-the-way-you-expect-it-to radiology"?

I'm not really sure what defines interventional radiology. It seems to include any procedure that involves a) the use of an imaging device for guidance of the procedure, and b) creating a new body orifice, either permanent or temporary. I'm thinking about starting an interventional radiology/dermatology practice. I examine the patients with a video camera and stick them with a pin, then I treat their acne.

My first interventional procedure was a renal cyst puncture. It was 1978, I was a first-year resident in Birmingham, Alabama, and Dr. Alan Tonkin walked me through the process of draining a cyst the size of a Volkswagen. I was scared to death I would miss, and I was shaking so badly I almost did.

Procedures on large renal cysts were very popular at the time, primarily because the equipment was so poor we couldn't see much else. We would drain them, fill them with air or contrast, sclerose them, and anything else we could imagine. The elusive tumor within a cyst was not going to get by us. It took several years to figure out how incredibly low the yield on such procedures was, and by then the equipment was improving enough to go on to bigger and bolder ideas.

After a long hiatus as a general medical officer in the Navy, I returned to radiology in 1983. While I was away, the scope of interventional procedures grew exponentially, and has continued to do so ever since. A lot of factors contributed to this growth. The primary reason is that these procedures are always done on someone else. How bold would "interventional pioneers" be if they were trying out new procedures on themselves?

Another obvious reason for the growth is the improvement in imaging technology. Biopsies are very difficult if you can see neither the target nor your biopsy device, although I have met more than one nephrologist who seemed convinced he could divine the right spot for a renal biopsy. Equipment manufacturers love this technology. The prices are outrageous, and by the time it is installed, it is outdated. MRI scanners are probably the only machines with a shorter half-life. They become "old-generation scanners" between the design and construction phase.

I'm convinced the real money is not in sales, but in service. You only buy complex angio-interventional equipment every few years, but it seems to need service every other week. You can buy a service contract (which allows your sales rep to retire early on the commission), or you can do your own in-house service. Of course, with only one real supplier, you can expect to get hosed every time you need a critical part.

When I entered private practice, I did basic interventional procedures—biopsies, drainage procedures, catheter placements, etc. Then we hired an interventionalist, a nurse, and three angio techs, and created an interventional radiology team. This has had several effects. The number and complexity of procedures have gone up, and the complication rate has gone down. A lung biopsy that used to tie up the scanner for forty-five minutes now takes two hours. The list of billing codes has grown like the number of nursing supervisors. And most importantly, I don't get called in for any of it.

An interesting part of interventional radiology is all the new gizmos. Everybody wants to create a gadget, especially something disposable that gets used several times a day by every lab in the country. Inventors like the royalties and, I suspect, the recognition that comes with designing a really popular instrument. Manufacturers and sales people love these new widgets, because every item is marked up about one million percent over cost.

Interventional radiology, like government, will continue to expand. They are always finding new ways to do old procedures as well as create solutions to problems previously thought insurmountable. A lot of nonradiologists feel threatened by this expansion, especially the surgeons who did the old procedures. Their practice and their income are declining, so they argue that these new procedures are not as good as "the old way." And once we prove that the new way really is better, they'll argue that it isn't radiology and they should be doing it.

To Boldly Go into the
Universe of Managed Care

One of the advantages (or disadvantages, depending on your perspective) of living in a rural area is that national trends tend to arrive late and leave later. We're still paying top dollar for Cabbage Patch Kids and LP records.

But I'm really excited because, as of January 1, my group has its first contract with a managed-care system. This has been looming as an inevitable landmark in my career, like my first barium enema blowout or my first severe contrast agent reaction. It's not that I think the old system was so equitable and perfect. I just hate health-insurance companies and their various mutant forms.

I'm not sure exactly why I dislike them so much. Perhaps it is their size, or the antagonistic role they always assume, or the huge power advantage they have over me and my patients. Maybe it is their bureaucracy, their mindless paperwork, or the frustration of knowing they get so much money for so little service.

Or maybe I'm just sick of the cheesy ad campaigns they are constantly producing with "healthcare dollars." If they feel compelled to throw away money, at least they could produce something as entertaining as a beer commercial.

Recently, I saw an HMO ad saying "Come be a part of our family." I thought their definition of a family must be a little different from mine. Or maybe not, since insurance companies act a lot like teen-age kids. They want your money on a regular basis, but when you occasionally ask for something in return, they give you twenty-five reasons why this is not the right time, place, or planet. For years I have been telling myself that my teen-agers will mature into reasonable, intelligent friends—so I shouldn't kill them. With HMOs and insurance companies I don't use that argument. I just can't seem to find the right lethal weapon.

Over the holidays I went to my first "Star Trek" flick: *First Contact*. If it had had a plot and some characters who knew how to act, it would have been a fair movie. Even without those nuances, the film hit home with me.

The good guys on the Starship Enterprise are battling the ultimate evil force in the universe, the Borg. Upon encountering an alien race, the Borg immediately tries to conquer it, and assimilate it into the collective being that is the Borg.

Once assimilated, you become a drone, existing only to benefit the Borg. While espousing a goal of perfection and universal oneness, the Borg functions entirely out of self-interest. Health-insurance company executives must idolize the Borg.

In his first term, President Clinton tried to reform healthcare. All the major players combined in an amazing display of greed, arrogance, and political ineptitude to produce nothing. This by default allowed corporate America to come up with our new, improved healthcare system—one based on profit instead of caring.

Providers and patients are like the people in the *Star Trek* film. From the moment assimilation begins, a mighty voice can be heard to say "Resistance is futile, resistance is futile…." America has created its own Borg. I can't run from it or hide. Scotty can't beam me up to safety.

I vaguely remember learning in a junior-high civics class that insurance was founded to share risks. Now, it seems that excluding risks and making profits are the primary goals. Payors want to assimilate as many doctors and patients as possible into their networks, but they expend endless energy and money trying to avoid their obligations to both groups.

For the past eight years, the insurer for about eighty percent of our patients has been Borg Cross/Borg Shield. Eight years in a row the premium for our group health insurance with "the Borgs" has gone up. And every one of those years BC/BS has lowered the professional fees they pay our group.

When I talk to other physicians, I learn that their fees are also going down, and everyone's insurance premiums are going up. What a great business. Expenses can be lowered, income and profits can be raised, and the only people who get pinched are the patients and providers for whom the whole system was established in the first place.

Sometimes fiction is more fun than life. In the movie, the Borg eventually assimilates the wrong being, and gets blown up from within. I enjoy contemplating this pleasant thought.

Our Work Is Important, but People Are More Important Still

Some days at work, things just seem a little off. Everyone needing a crosstable lateral C-spine has shoulders that go up to their ears. The ER is running a special on V/Q scans and leg vein ultrasounds for patients with the body and cooperation of Godzilla. Every diagnostic mammo needs mag views, so the schedule is way behind.

I have a well-developed technique for handling these snags in the radiological day: I whine. But it never fails—when I moan about little problems all day, I diagnose a malignancy in someone my own age or younger, and suddenly I'm reminded what real problems are.

One Friday a few months ago I was having a hectic night on call. The ER was swamped. One of their primary techniques for creating space seems to be ordering every test available, because a patient in nuclear medicine, ultrasound, or CT is a patient not in the ER. I, of course, was whining loudly, when I got a call saying my mother in Alabama was very ill. Catching a plane Saturday morning got very important, and handling the onslaught from the ER got very easy.

I made my flight (it left late) and my connection in Atlanta (a long airport run), so I got to Mobile by noon. That afternoon my mother and I spent the last six hours of her life holding hands. Not a long time in the course of one's life, but it did and still does seem important. It also reminded me that, as a radiologist, I deal daily with serious and fatal diagnoses, but seldom with physical death.

For the first time in my life I had to arrange a funeral, and a whole new set of things became important. Caskets, cemetery plots, calling relatives, obituaries, and all the trappings of death had to be handled. So I found myself at midnight Sunday talking long distance on the phone, asking a friend who knows such things how to iron my mother's favorite chiffon dress without burning it to a crisp. In life, my mother was very particular about her clothes. I don't know about clothes and death, but I wasn't going to take any chances.

By the time of the visitation Monday afternoon at the funeral home, I thought I had things under control. A little old lady friend of my mother's told me there was an error in her obituary. Contrary to what it said in the paper, my mother was never a member of the Daughters of the American Revolution, but she was a devoted member of the United Daughters of the Confederacy. It didn't seem like an important mistake until the fourth little old lady pointed it out to me. Never in my wildest dreams did I imagine "the Confederacy" would ever be important to me. I had the newspaper print a correction the next day.

The funeral was Tuesday. A lot of people came and a lot of nice things were said about my mother. Being in the town where I was raised meant seeing lots of old friends of mine and my family. I said, "Good to see you again. Thank you for coming" about 3,000 times. I really wanted to remember their names, but it's something I have never been good at, especially under stress. They had the home court advantage on remembering my name, since they knew whose funeral they were attending.

I spent Wednesday filling a U-Haul with everything I thought might someday be important to me or my kids from my mother's estate. That will really make you assess your priorities. Interestingly, my mom had endured hundreds of imaging studies during her five-year illness, but I never considered saving one of them. Our work is important, but only for the moment.

Thursday I drove 850 miles home. It seemed like a good omen when the radio played "Six Days on the Road and I'm Gonna Make It Home Tonight" before I was out of Alabama. There are times, when I'm focused on problems at the hospital, that I dream about chucking it for a less stressful job. I actually enjoy mindless drives on the interstate, so long-distance trucking has crossed my mind. But when you talk to truckers, or anyone else who has a job, you realize everyone has frustrations at work. We just get paid better for ours.

Friday I was back in the hospital. There were the usual slightly misexposed films, patients who couldn't be positioned just right, and children who wouldn't stop moving. But none of them made me whine. The details are important. The people, patients and co-workers, are more important.

RSNA Makes Mickey Mouse Move
by Exiting Chicago

After months of negotiation, the Radiological Society of North America is moving its annual meeting to Orlando, Florida—sort of.

The board decided to move the meeting to the Sunshine State for 2002 and 2003, back to Chicago in '04, and then alternate yearly after that. Personally, I have a hard time buying my Christmas presents on time, so I can't conceive of my plans for 2002.

How does this affect the average radiologist, if such a beast exists? At the moment, not at all. Most radiologists are more concerned with how or if they'll be getting paid to do radiology in 2002, not where the RSNA meeting will be held. But it means a lot to the city of Chicago, which will lose between $70 million and $100 million in income from the show. It also probably means a lot to the manufacturers, who plan much of their marketing year around the meeting.

There are a few things that come to mind when I contemplate the move. For one thing, we'll all look better in Orlando. Families and guests of the attendees (and probably more than a few of those attending) will be sporting poolside tans by the end of the week. People will be wearing casual clothes, instead of dead-animal coats, which seem to be the rage in Chicago. And everyone will have normal-looking hair. Every day is a bad hair day in a city as windy as Chicago.

Christmas shopping will no longer be an entertaining diversion, unless everyone in your family wants something with a mouse on it. Well, this isn't entirely true. Like most resorts, Orlando has become a haven for outlet shoppers. These are people who think if they go into a chain store with the word "outlet" in the title, they are getting a bargain.

Chicago is famous for its pizza. Oranges come to mind when I think of Central Florida. I was in Orlando in February at the annual Johns Hopkins CT meeting. (I've attended this meeting a couple of times and I always learn some new things.) I ended up eating lunch one day at Pizzeria Uno, so now I don't have to go to Chicago for its famous pizza. Of course, it has about as much authenticity as believing you're in Italy when you eat in an Olive Garden.

Chicago's Magnificent Mile is a street I really like, although it should be called the "Decadent Mile." Seeing all those lights, all those window displays, and all the freezing people can't help but get you in the Christmas spirit. Shorts and a tan will be nice in November, but they're not the same.

Hotel rooms seem to be the big factor in the RSNA's decision. Chicago hotel managers were becoming less willing to hold their rooms at convention rates (never a real bargain from my small-town perspective) when they could let them at exorbitant rates once the rooms reserved for the convention were gone. I think the RSNA did its members a big service by concentrating on this point, since for us, this is the major expense of the meeting. One year I paid about $100 a night for a single bed in a closet at the Drake Hotel. Of course, it was a very handsome closet.

There are also the added benefits that come with holding the meeting so close to the Disney empire. While you're in the meeting, your family will be able to spend massive amounts of money in the Disney theme parks. You may even be able to take advantage of Disney's newest method of entertaining you while siphoning your wallet: the Disney Institute. This place is particularly interesting since it will now have an incentive to design courses specifically for radiologists, such as the following:

• *Increasing Your BE Referral Rate.* How to make them feel like they've been for a ride on Space Mountain.

• *Animated CT Scans.* Give your referring physicians images they can really understand.

• *Virtual Radiology.* How to do procedures on patients who don't exist, and who to bill for them.

• *Always a Happy Ending.* Taught by former Disney executives, this course tells how you can earn millions of dollars by screwing up your job and getting fired.

It isn't too surprising that the RSNA meeting is going to be bouncing back and forth between two cities. The meeting has long suffered from an identity conflict: Is it a scientific assembly or is it a trade show? And remember, this decision was made by a group of radiologists.

They hedged.

Sometimes You Can't Avoid Working in the Gray Zone

"A radiologist with a ruler is a dangerous man." I heard that in 1978, my first year in radiology training. Seldom does a day go by that I don't think of it. We are constantly following up on or intervening in cases where patients have violated some arbitrary measurement, either on an X-ray or on lab work.

Of course, there are times when exact measurements are critical. But as radiologists we are dealing with the human body, and most bodies haven't read the books that quote precise measurements.

When I trained, I learned that a normal common bile duct measures up to 7 mm. The calipers on our ultrasound machine go to tenths of a millimeter. I felt very precise. After a while, though, I began to see that some people who aren't sick have ducts larger than 7 mm. Then one day Dr. Roger Sanders told me he liked to use about a millimeter's width for each decade of the patient's age. My kind of rule: It varies with age, and begins with "about."

Some radiologists (and people in general) seem obsessed with measuring and counting everything they come upon. I trained with a really nice guy who had to organize and quantify everything. Our study carrels were next to each other and we sometimes drove each other crazy. My desk would always be a mess, while his was pristine. Even the paper clips in his drawer were lined up precisely. Periodically, I would trash his desk. These attempts to help him loosen up were not greatly appreciated. But even he cracked when I put EZ Gas crystals in his hat—a unique sensation when your head starts to sweat.

Mammography is an area where this numbers game can really drive you crazy. We are constantly chasing 3-mm ditzels that may or may not have been 2.5-mm ditzels on the last mammo. As resolution has improved, this has gotten more and more involved. Some days I miss xeromammography; it was easier when I couldn't see.

Microcalcifications are another numbers nightmare. Just how many microcalcifications are in a cluster? I attended Marc Homer's excellent course in Boston on a practical approach to mammography. He spent a while discussing how different experts arbitrarily define a cluster and how ultimately we each have to pick which definition we are going to use. But a pearl I really liked was to call a group of calcifications less than a cluster by some other name, such as "a focus of calcifications." That is more on my thought level: "Cluster" bad; "focus" good. Unfortunately, I still have to count them.

One of the nephrologists in our hospital brought me an article about adult renal cystic disease. The authors believed that the diagnosis of polycystic disease was being underdiagnosed, and that the exact number of cysts in every adult kidney needed to be counted and reported in any imaging study of the kidneys. This makes perfect sense to a nephrologist, since as a group they are the most anal-retentive specialists on earth. I told him our group would discuss it, but you can be sure he doesn't want to hear what was said.

A popular measurement I have always found interesting is the cardiac to thoracic width ratio. I have known many fine radiologists who routinely include this on their chest dictations. Like so many things we do in radiology, it seems to be a function of where you train.

Part of my training was at the University of Alabama in Birmingham. At the time, the faculty included a noted pulmonary radiologist and an equally published cardiac radiologist. They got along like Clinton and Gingrich. Like any intelligent first-year resident, I was a fervent supporter of whoever's service I was on at the time. On the pulmonary service I waxed poetic about the pulmonary interstitium, while on the cardiac service I described every detail relevant to cardiac physiology. No azygos vein, atrial appendage, or upper lobe vessel felt slighted. Neither one taught me the nuances of the C/T ratio, so I don't report it.

Reporting numbers is often unavoidable. Our oncologists seem to want monthly measurements of every node in the county. But most of the measurements we report are points on a continuum, and the difference between normal and abnormal is always a gray zone. Some of the most challenging and satisfying work I do is in this gray zone. Unfortunately, it is also where I sometimes look the dumbest, and then it gets chalked up to experience.

The Good, Bad, and Ugly
of Everyday Practice

Like most things that are important in life, my relationship with radiology is a love/hate situation. Throughout the day there are little things that make me smile or frown and determine my satisfaction with work and myself.

I really like UGI and BE air-contrast films that work. They have a certain aesthetic quality that has appeal beyond their diagnostic value.

I like all the good food our techs bring in to celebrate a birthday, a wedding, a departure, a sunrise, and so forth.

I like MR images that demonstrate cranial nerve anatomy in minute detail. I loved learning them in medical school, and prior to MRI all the tests we did involved more imagination than knowledge. I should apologize personally to all the people I put through an air-contrast CT of their acoustic nerve.

The older I get, the less I like being on call. It is particularly distressing to be finishing up a long day's work, and have an ultrasound or CT tech come up and ask, "Are you the doctor on call tonight?"

I like knowing that from any window in our hospital, you can see cows out in the pastures, or fields of cultivated farmland. I'm less keen on the fact that a few times a year in our department, you can smell the output of the former being spread to increase the output of the latter.

I love it when I'm on call and the CT scanner blows a tube at five o'clock. Sure, I feel bad that all those headaches in the ER have to wait until morning, but I don't lose sleep over it.

I hate it when the fluoro machine goes down in the middle of an exam. It's not my fault, but that isn't what's written all over the patient's face. And "Tipler" is the only name he or she is going to remember.

I like fatty breasts—when I'm doing mammography.

I hate finding my own mistakes, and I really hate having someone else finding them and showing them to me.

I love hitting one out of the park. A patient has obscure symptoms, the referring physician presents the case, I suggest a diagnosis and a test to confirm it, and I'm right! I just wish it happened more often.

I hate BEs that blow out on the table. I feel guilty not helping clean up a mess that I obviously helped create—but not guilty enough to stay.

I hate days that run beyond ten hours. It is definitely possible to get too much of a good thing.

I like doing a breast biopsy of a mass under ultrasound and hitting a cyst. It feels good to say "This is nothing to worry about. Have a nice weekend." And you know, that woman, who probably hasn't slept well since she scheduled the biopsy, is going to appreciate all the little things in her life for the next day or two more than she ever thought possible.

I like color-flow Doppler of painful testicles. Nuclear medicine never let me down in that situation; it was just so indirect and nonspecific that I sweated bullets until the boy was surgerized, or his pain responded to antibiotics.

I like thyroid disease, when the patient has read the textbook. But about ten percent of these patients have not done their reading. I would prefer these patients go to the university.

I hate venograms on massively swollen legs. Actually, I dislike massively swollen legs in general.

I like patients who know the difference between "scoot to your left" and "turn to your left."

I dislike whiny adults who make a big deal out of drinking a little barium.

To paraphrase Robert Duvall, "I love the smell of barium in the morning."

I like clean colons, but I don't tell that to people outside of radiology.

I dislike procedures on macho young men—they always faint.

I love obstetrical ultrasound, but I hate diagnosing fetal demise.

I dread the prospect of having emergency-medicine residents in our ER twenty-four hours a day. They start in a few months, and I know our call is going to go from bad to terrible.

I hate reading and signing someone else's reports, and I'm not real keen on doing my own.

I hate having my beeper go off when I have just walked out of the hospital, just sat down for dinner, just climbed into the sack, just gotten into an amorous situation, or just about any time at all.

Rereading this list, I realize the problems in my day aren't all that bad, and there is some truth in the old saying, "Simple pleasures for simple people."

It's Not All Downhill at Wyoming Ski Meeting

Shortly after moving to Virginia ten years ago, my kids and I took up snow skiing. We live about thirty minutes from Virginia's two largest downhill ski areas, so group lessons were cheap and easy. My progress could be summed up with an expression I use at work: "I may be slow, but I'm not any good."

Over the years I actually did improve, a little. But with age comes wisdom, or at least the recognition of one's mortality. So I switched to telemark and cross-country skiing, and my kids do both. Here the speeds are slower, the pace more controlled, and the settings far less crowded. Being out in the woods cross-country skiing with my kids is, for me, the epitome of "quality time." At least for the first part of the day. Then their youthful bodies start to run me into the ground, and I approach "coronary time."

Downhill skiing in Virginia is slightly better than in Florida. Cross-country skiing in Virginia is beautiful, when there is snow. That is the crux of the problem. We don't have enough real snow, so they make artificial snow every night at the downhill areas. Then every day it turns to ice and a lot of the people sliding down the slopes end up in my department. "What," you might ask, "does this have to do with radiology?" (Other than the fact that these icy slopes are good for my department's numbers.)

In the eastern half of the United States, if you ski or talk about skiing, there is always someone who starts going on about the skiing "out West." If you have never skied out West, these people sound obnoxious. But a few years ago my daughter and I finally went for a week of skiing in Colorado. Now I have yet another attribute that makes me obnoxious. It is amazing, though, what you can stumble on when you aren't even trying.

Now every year we plan a trip out West. In an effort to combine work with fun, and shortchange the IRS, I attend a CME course. I have always chosen the course based on strict criteria: my daughter's school schedule and the quality of the skiing. Last winter this led me to Jackson Hole, Wyoming, and Dr. Patricia Weber's "Current Diagnostic Imaging in the Hole" course. What a find.

Jackson is an amazing place to ski. All the other attendees at the course were gravity slaves, and they said the downhill skiing was wonderful. Looking at the mountains, I'm sure they were right. For cross-country and back-country skiing, the area is equally wonderful. I intend to go back this year, not because this is the only great place to ski, but because the meeting turned out to be unique.

What makes the Jackson meeting interesting is the presence of two separate faculties. Four published authorities in separate areas of radiology gave lectures each day. Towards the end of the day three equally noted authorities in those same fields critiqued the lectures given earlier. While done in good spirit, and with a lot of humor, there were some significant differences of opinion. This is very useful to an "average" radiologist like me.

When I go to a meeting, it is often hard not to get caught up in what a good speaker sees as the best way to do something. I don't get quite as enthusiastic as those idiots you see on infomercials for car wax and toilet cleaners—but I can come pretty close.

Sometimes, when I get home, things just don't seem to go as well in my hands as they seemed to for the speaker. For example, I am ready to quit going to lectures on shoulder ultrasound. What looks and sounds straightforward in the lectures is not very reliable with me holding the transducer. If you want me to tell you what is wrong with your shoulder, you need a needle, or an MRI, or better still, both. So it was nice in Wyoming to hear an expert say, "Hey, I tried what you were talking about this morning, and it didn't do diddly."

There are at least two positive things that happen to me when I hear experts disagree about a technique. First, it makes me a little more cautious about giving up the way of doing things that I know and feel comfortable using. But more importantly, if and when I screw up something while using this new method, I don't feel quite so stupid. The old adage is true that misery loves company.

So come the first week of February, I hope I'll be in Jackson Hole. I'm looking forward to some good skiing, some good food (I never go anywhere twice that doesn't have good food), and watching some good radiologists mix it up at the podium.

Providing Good Service Just Isn't Enough These Days

The practice of radiology can no longer be thought of simply as a specialty in medicine. All manner of consultants and managerial professionals tell us we must think of ourselves as a "service industry." We are the providers, serving two sets of customers: our patients and their referring physicians. Our practice patterns must reflect this new mentality; change is inevitable.

Always hoping to stay current in radiology, I try to incorporate this new perspective into my work. However, it becomes difficult during those times when I am wrestling with the urge to strangle a fellow physician.

Just a few days ago, a local internist came down to review the chest X-ray on one of his inpatients. Trailing him like an admiring puppy was a young medical student. This physician is a friend of mine, I give him lots of money when we play poker together, and yet he ignored me as I sat just a few feet away. They found the patient they were looking for on the multi-viewer, and the physician began to wax poetic about the subtleties on the chest film. This was particularly ironic, since from my perspective, he was missing most of those subtleties.

I didn't know whether to correct him, ignore him, or choke him. "Aha!' I told myself. "We are a service industry. I will not strangle this arrogant fool today. Maybe next time, but not today."

The student is not my customer. If he chooses to acquire his radiologic acumen from a general internist or a lawn chair, that is outside my sphere of influence. Hopefully, he will develop the necessary discrimination skills to identify a black pearl when he hears one. The doctor will know what I think about the chest film when he reads my report. So I bite my tongue, and learn to enjoy being part of a service industry.

This medical-student ego trip is relatively new for us. Our little hospital is about forty-five minutes from a major university hospital. Our administration is constantly developing ways to "partner" and "network" with the university. This is hospital administration lingo for "avoid being swallowed immediately." Recent innovations include university residents in our ER, and medical students rotating with our medical staff. Given the seemingly endless supply of administrators in our hospital, I'm sure there is one somewhere trying to figure out how to partner in radiology.

There are a few other referring physicians who have a way of pushing my desire to serve near its limit. Our department has a turnaround time on reports of about four hours. I think this is good. We also have a digital dictation system which allows immediate recall of our dictation by any physician with access to a phone. And yet, we still have a small group of doctors who write "call wet reading" on just about every exam they order. It is almost part of their signature. I am tempted to ask them if they give immediate appointments, consults, and opinions to all their customers. But, as a happy member of a service industry, I just write out the wet reading for the tech to call.

I could write a whole column about unreasonable demands from the ER—in fact I did. Boy, did I get some spicy faxes from ER staff around the country. Contrary to what I see on TV, there are a lot of humor-impaired ER docs out there. But, as a happy member of a service industry, I just try to accommodate their demands for instant radiology.

There is a special group of physicians who have a way of testing everyone in our department. They like to be very specific in the way they request exams, because they think they know everything. When the tech and/or the radiologist does the exam slightly different than requested, these physicians have to come down and yell at someone. They strut into the department (I don't know why, but these people like to strut) and make some sweeping inane command like, "I never want my orders changed. If you can't get what I ordered, call me and I'll show you what I want." Usually, it is obvious to everyone what they requested, but either it just isn't possible in the patient, or what they want is stupid. As members of a service industry we smile, explain what we did, and thank them for their offer to help in the future. We all really want help from people who don't even know how dumb they're acting.

Actually, I think everyone in my department tries to provide the best service possible. I'm proud of the job we do. I just get aggravated by the few physicians who take advantage of our willingness to help. Fortunately, I'm not to the point of some other service industry personnel—postal workers.

There Is No Greater Luxury
Than a Fine Whine

"Life is hard." This is one of life's truths. I try to remind myself of this when the going gets rough. It seems that for some people, however, life is really hard—or at least they are constantly saying it is. How do you tell the folks who are truly having a lot of hard luck from the ones who just want you to think they are?

You might be a whiner if your X-ray film jacket weighs almost as much as you do, and they're all normal studies.

You might be a whiner if you show up for your pelvic ultrasound demanding the receptionist take you right back for the scan, and your bladder is empty.

You might be a whiner if you start complaining about the compression on your mammogram before the tech starts to lower the paddle.

You might be a whiner if you make a technologist repeat a portable film more than three times because you're not satisfied with the technique.

You might be a whiner if you come to the ER after midnight for symptoms you have had for more than a month.

You might be a whiner if you are a second- or third-shift technologist, and you call in your backup tech more than all the other techs on that shift combined.

You might be a whiner if you spend as much time complaining about the service you are covering that day as you do dictating the exams.

You might be a whiner if you insist on being premedicated for a BE

You might be a whiner if you show up for an exam on the wrong day, the staff works you in, and then you complain about having to wait.

You might be a whiner if the techs don't like to call you in at night because you make such a big deal about it on the phone.

You might be a whiner if you're having an upper GI because you haven't been able to keep anything down for months, and there is a question about whether you exceed the weight limit on the fluoro table.

You might be a whiner if you complain about the techs paging you, when they've been waiting twenty minutes for you to review an exam.

You might be a whiner if you complain about the coffee pot being empty when you want some, but you don't make a pot when you drink the last cup.

You might be a whiner if you complain about add-ons to the fluoro schedule when you're doing the work, but don't think twice about approving a case for someone else's Saturday morning case load.

You might be a whiner if you come to the ER because your fingers are blue. I actually saw a teen-age girl for this when I was an ER doctor. She was referred by her school nurse, who found "cyanosis" in a book under the differential for blue fingers. She and her mother waited two hours. My eventual diagnosis was "new Levis."

You might be a whiner if every time the ER orders a study you don't feel like doing, you complain about the quality of the emergency-room doctors. This is especially true between midnight and 7:30 A.M., a period when I get particularly critical of their clinical acumen.

You might be a whiner if you're a young guy with a sprained ankle, but you're complaining and yelling more than the seventy-year-old woman in the next room with a hip fracture.

You might be a whiner if you're a surgeon who complains things never look right on the C-arm because the techs don't know what they're doing.

You might be a whiner if you come to the ER after a huge Thanksgiving dinner for "diffuse stomach pain." Score double whiner points if you wait until after the ball games are over before you come. The ER doctor gets quadruple wimp points if he or she really needs a CT to be sure the patient is safe to send home.

You might be a whiner if you want your wife in the room when you have an upper GI.

You might be a whiner if you never like the food in your hospital cafeteria, or maybe you just have functioning taste buds.

You might be a whiner if you're a cardiologist who complains about the occasional patient with a false-positive myocardial perfusion scan, but ignores all the negative caths done for "clinical indications."

You might be a whiner if you work in medicine, where you see people daily who are suffering or struggling to stay alive, and you aren't thankful that you can enjoy all the challenges and variety you get to deal with every day.

Truth Is Nice, but It Pales
In Comparison to the Law

Being in the medical field has its rewards and its punishments. People involved with radiology-doctors and techs alike-have to deal with some of the downside factors on a frequent basis. Perhaps the one that bothers me the most is having to deal with the dregs of society. We get these scumbags as patients, or accompanying patients, and they make our work more complicated for no good reason.

At times these feelings inspire guilt in me. I have to remind myself that I took an oath to take care of all people, even the bottom-feeders. We are professionals, so I hold my breath and, as quickly as possible, I deal with lawyers.

Lawyers have become a pervasive part of U.S. society. This is because we produce them at about the same rate as cornflakes, only with less quality control. My own state of Virginia now graduates more lawyers annually than the entire continent of Europe.

When an attorney, or the relative of a prominent local attorney, comes into our ER, everyone gets excited. Before the patient ever gets to us, someone has let us know we will be getting "one of them." I see a sort of poetic justice in this. There is probably no better way to get people to screw up than to make them extremely anxious about a task they would routinely do with little concern.

I don't even like getting mail from attorneys. If it is a letter from my own attorney, I know I will eventually be billed for the paper, envelope, postage, and ten times the amount of time it took to write the letter. If the envelope has some other law office on the outside, I get anxious. A silent prayer goes up: "Please let this be a disability claim."

A lot of my friends from college went to law school. They were good people, but law school changed them. It altered their perspective. I know some lawyers now, and most of them are good people too. But they all have this same crazy orientation. What matters is *the law.*

Truth is nice, justice is a fine concept, fairness sounds pretty good in theory—but all else pales in comparison to *the law*. Imagine if doctors took that kind of stance. "I'm sorry you feel bad, Mrs. Smith. I would like to put you in the hospital and make you feel better, but I have to think first of *the hospital.*" Doctors aren't trained that way; at least, they weren't in the past.

Perhaps this is one of the reasons medicine is evolving as it is. We live in a country governed predominantly by lawyers, who are used to thinking of an institution as more important than the individual. Having been trained the opposite way, it is no wonder we find it hard to change.

Not all lawyers elicit such a violent gag reflex from me. Our group's lawyer is much more tolerable. He comes down once a year to our corporate meeting and passes around a lot of meaningless official memos for us to sign. This keeps us in compliance with the latest changes in the tax laws, which other lawyers in Washington have made in order to produce revenue for their law firm—at home.

I was involved in the merger of two radiology groups. We had numerous meetings where the members of our groups met to discuss the details of our merger contract. Our corporate lawyer was there, answering the occasional legal question. When he wasn't answering questions, I kept having mental images of a gas pump. I could almost see his eyes moving in a vertical nystagmus as the dollars clicked away by the minute, faster than pennies on a real gas pump.

The ones that really gripe me are the plaintiffs' lawyers. Why is a lawyer entitled to fifty percent of someone' compensation for misfortune? I don't get fifty percent of my patients' income if I diagnose their medical problems. Their primary physicians don't get fifty percent of their income for keeping them healthy throughout the year. Doctors would try all kinds of long shots if they knew a) they got half the patient's income if they were right, and b) they only lost a little time if they weren't. No more list of differentials for me; I give one shot from the hip, and if I'm right once or twice a year, I'm home free.

I suspect some of my problem is the old green-eyed monster: envy. If radiologists controlled Congress, there would probably be laws requiring every adult in the country to have annual BEs, mammograms-ever the men-UGIs, chest X-rays, and multiple nuclear scans. (Nuclear docs seem to have a special touch with Congress.) To my mind, this would seem rational, in spite of the additional work and income it would force on me and my partners.

Dr. Brad Meets HAL In 2007
—A Radiology Odyssey

A handsome young doctor sits in the only chair in a large dark room with a bank of high-resolution monitors on one wall. A waltz is playing in the background. He addresses the wall in a soft voice.

"Good morning, HAL. How are you this morning?"

"Good morning, Brad. I'm doing very well today. And you?" says the wall, in an equally soft but somewhat monotonic voice.

"I'm fine, HAL. Are you ready to get started?" he says.

"Of course, Brad. The GE 9000 High Amplified Lamore total-body scanner is always ready to scan. We are one hundred percent operational one hundred percent of the time. Our limiting factor is the humans that operate us."

"Thank you for reminding me, HAL. Bring up the first patient."

The wall is filled with a series of images resembling the data from the Visible Human Project. There are also several monitors showing total-body spectroscopy peaks.

"Brad, you're looking at the data set on Mrs. T. Beauregard Jones, a forty-five YOWF in for her annual."

"Thank you, HAL. Bring in her GI tract, please."

The central screens fill with images of the intestinal tract from the mouth to the anus.

"HAL, the mucosal surfaces are not clear. Can you sharpen them up for me?"

"I'm sorry, Brad. I'm afraid I can't do that," says the wall.

"Why not, HAL?"

"The credentials committee met last night and made a final decision on the case presented to the administration by the gastroenterologists. Since their scopes used to be the best way to see it, the committee decided they are the doctors who should evaluate the mucosa. I'll be glad to zoom in on everything below the basement membrane for you, Brad."

"That's okay, HAL. I trained evaluating the mucosal surfaces by indirect methods. Just show me the air in the lumen," says Brad. "Thank you, HAL. That looks fine. Can you bring up her vascular system for me?"

In an instant, an MRA of the entire vascular system fills the main screens. The heart is absent.

"HAL, we seem to be missing a little detail."

"Very observant, Brad. You probably noticed the heart isn't here. Actually, the heart and 1.5 cm of the ascending aorta have been deleted. I'm afraid your scores on the cardiac CAQ last week weren't quite up to snuff. Perhaps a little more study and you can bring it up on next month's exam. What do you think of her arch?"

"It looks pretty good to me. Is this a test, HAL?"

"I agree, Brad. The arch looks normal. And yes, Ms. Helga Wilmut, R.N., chief of radiology, has asked me to audit your performance. T. B. Price, R.N., chief of the medical staff, requested it in the interest of the hospital. Do you have a problem with this, Brad?"

"No, HAL, I don't have a problem. I believe in the hospital's policy of continuous quality assessment. Tell me, who is monitoring nurse Wilmut and nurse Price?"

"They monitor each other. And they report to each other at their twice-daily monitoring meetings. They also meet daily with the nurse supervisors, the nurse team leaders, the nursing coordinators, the nurse department heads, and the individual department nurses and nursing liaisons. As your personal scanner, I report my findings and your interpretations to seventeen different nurse administrators. Not to mention the federal agency and private insurance nurse liaisons who monitor our output. Don't worry, Brad. When you speak, people listen."

"That's very reassuring, HAL. Do my readings still go to the patient's personal doctor?"

"Well, not exactly. They go to the doctor's nurse. The doctor's nurse and the patient's payor nurse liaison then decide if the results are worth remunerating, and if so, your findings are transferred on to the doctor."

"I need to get back to work, HAL. It looks to me like we need to biopsy Mrs. Jones' liver. Would you call the technologists doing biopsies today?"

"Brad, I don't think you want to say that. You know how upset the technicians get when you call them technologists."

"You're right, HAL. Old habits die hard."

The screens show two RTs arriving in the adjacent large scanning room, where Mrs. Jones lies on a scanner bed. In about ten minutes, they biopsy a 2-cm lesion near the diaphragm in the right lobe of her liver as the doctor watches on a monitor.

"HAL, the biopsy went very well. I think we're through with Mrs. Jones for today. Would you have her come into my office? I want to go over the results with her."

"I'll be glad to, Brad. The hospital retail products liaison nurse has asked me to remind you that your figures last month were down. Your withhold is in jeopardy. As I'm sure you remember, patient consultation time is your prime opportunity to boost your monthly sales figures. You do want to make the HMO's premier physician list."

"Thank you for reminding me, HAL. I don't want to forget what being a doctor is all about."

About the Author

Dr. Brad Tipler has been in the private practice of radiology for the last ten years. His hospital-based practice is in the Shenandoah Valley of Virginia. He attended medical school at the University of Alabama in Birmingham, Alabama, and did his internship there as well. After spending five years as a general medical officer in the U.S. Navy (the first year was at the Navy's request, the next four were just fun), Brad did a radiology residency at the National Naval Medical Center in Bethesda, Maryland. Although he is constantly poking fun at them, he is a proud member of the American College of Radiology and the Radiological Society of North America.